"But Don't All Religions Lead to God?"

Navigating the Multi-faith Maze

Michael Green

Baker Books

A Division of Baker Book House Co
Grand Rapids, Michigan 49516

Published by Baker Books
a division of Baker Book House Company
P.O. Box 6287, Grand Rapids, MI 49516-6287

Printed in the United States of America

Library of Congress Cataloging-in-Publication Data is on file at the Library of Congress, Washington, D.C.

ISBN 0-8010-6439-2

For current information about all releases from Baker Book House, visit our web site:
                    http://www.bakerbooks.com

For Tim,
working at the interface
with other religions.

Contents

Introduction

I was sitting recently in my pajamas talking with fellow patients in a hospital ward, having just had a heart attack. We were chatting about Jesus, as it happened. The prevailing view among my friends there was that all religions are much the same, and in any case we can rely on any or all of them leading to God.

Returning from hospital I had a phone call from a long-time friend who visits in prisons. He told me of four experimental Kainos wings run on Christian principles, which are by far the most successful in preventing reoffending. They are under threat of closure by the Home Office. Why? On the grounds that Christianity is no different from any other religion and must be given no privileged position: all faiths must be treated alike. Can anything be more crazy when the country is crying out for a way to prevent reoffending by discharged prisoners? As one Chaplain put it, "We are being sacrificed on the altar of multi-faith political correctness".

Another friend who is a teacher expressed her surprise that some of the assemblies at school were being given over the Buddhism. "Well, all religions lead to God, so why not give our students the choice?" responded the Head.

It seemed to me that there was a bit of confusion out there.

So I wrote this book. I deliberately kept it short so that you will have time to read it: it is an important subject on which there is a lot of muddled thinking.

Enjoy it!

Michael Green
Christmas 2001
(or should I have said the Winter Festival,
or the Saturnalia? No doubt they are all the same!)

Chapter 1

"It Doesn't Matter What You Believe As Long As You Are Sincere"

[handwritten margin notes: liberal / to P.C. / (crowd does / believe this it / often areas]

That is something you often hear when religion is being discussed. Not, of course, when the talk is about politics or whether one country should bomb another. You never hear it when people are talking about the horrors of Auschwitz or Belsen. Hitler was undoubtedly sincere in his hatred of the Jewish people, but everyone would admit he was wrong. (If you don't admit it, I shall take leave to disbelieve you!) The massacre of six million Jews in the Second World War was deliberate, ruthless, and the product of a very clear and sincerely held belief. Hitler was sincere but terribly wrong.

[handwritten margin notes: to folly / ; to eda]

An example like this, which caused the annihilation of millions of people, should make us very cautious about claiming that it does not matter what you believe as long as you are sincere. It is manifestly nonsense. For centuries people sincerely believed that thunder was caused by the gods at war. We now know that this sincerely held belief was superstitious rubbish. They were sincere but wrong. For centuries people sincerely believed that the sun went around the earth. When Galileo, following Copernicus, showed this was not the case, he was forbidden by the pope

9

to "hold, teach or defend" such a view and was handed over to the Inquisition. I am sure he would not have agreed, as he languished in his prison, that it does not matter what you believe as long as you are sincere!

Now, of course, sincerity is vitally important. Everyone dislikes a hypocrite. But sincerity is not enough. I may sincerely believe that all airplanes at London Airport will take me to America, but I would be wrong. I may sincerely believe that lots of cream and chocolate is the best way to recuperate after a heart attack, but I would be wrong.

If the notion that sincerity is all you need is manifestly ridiculous, why do people say it so often when the subject of religion is raised? There may be several reasons.

For one thing, people may simply not want to get drawn into a religious argument. They know that these are fruitless, and so they try to avoid an embarrassing and perhaps acrimonious discussion by claiming that it doesn't matter what you believe as long as you are sincere.

Others make the claim, I think, because they have never really stopped to think. They would never say it about a historical topic like World War Two: you may sincerely believe Hitler won, but you would be mistaken. They would never apply it to mathematics: nobody in their right mind imagines that if only they believe hard enough that two and two equals five, that would make it so. However great your sincerity, you would be wrong. No, it is only in the area of religion that people talk like this, perhaps because it is so hard to achieve certainty in religion. The topic is as slippery as soap in water. Much better, then, to duck out of the subject altogether and airily suggest that it does not matter what you believe as long as you are sincere.

Another reason may be this, at least in the UK and USA: we are practical people. We are *not* famous for our philosophical thinking. If something works, it is OK, no matter who invented it or what he intended. As a race, we are concerned with actions, not with theories. So it is not difficult to carry that attitude a bit further and maintain, "It does not matter what you believe as long as you are sincere."

But I fancy there is a deeper reason. Religion is about the fundamental issues of life and death, and there is something in us that does not want to look at them. They feel rather spooky and uncomfortable. We would rather live for the here and now and shut our eyes to complex matters like life and death, heaven and hell. Much easier to rely on sincerity and living a reasonably decent life, in the hope that this will carry us through.

This attitude is very widespread. I found myself chatting to a fellow patient in the hospital on just this very matter recently, and he listened with some interest to the story of Jesus, to His offer and His challenge on our lives – and then he smiled, shrugged his shoulders and made it clear that the topic was uncomfortable. I asked him if he would like to look at a brief account of the evidence for who Jesus was and what He had done for humankind, and he declined. I told him of a monthly Men's Breakfast (at which I had recently spoken) in his home town, and suggested I might get him an invitation. But no, thanks. "I don't think it matters what you believe as long as you are sincere."

Where does this leave us? Well, the teachings of Buddha and the teachings of Jesus point in fundamentally different directions. You may be a sincere follower of the Buddha, but what if that allegiance should prove in the end to be mistaken? You may be sincere in thinking Jesus Christ is out of date and anyhow, He was merely a good man. But what if you happen to be sincere and wrong? What if God should meet you at the end of the road and ask, "Why did you not bother about My Son Jesus who gave Himself to put you right with Me?" Will you mumble, "Oh well, I thought that it couldn't matter what I believed as long as I was sincere"? The fact is that belief is the spring of action, and right belief the spring of right action. We cannot escape into "sincerity". Sincerity is absolutely essential but, by itself, absolutely insufficient. We would never apply that argument to any other area of life: it is madness to apply it to religion. So let us turn in the next chapter to the substantial issue: are all religions much the same?

Chapter 2

"Aren't All Religions Much the Same?"

"Globalization" is one of the current buzz words, drawing attention to the fact that our world is closely inter-connected. What happens in one part, like Bosnia or Afghanistan, affects the rest of the world. The pop music from America is played just as enthusiastically in China and India. Our world is a global village, and we are increasingly realizing it. So when it comes to religion we are not at all surprised to find Jews and Sikhs, Muslims, Buddhists and Hindus mingling in our streets and staffing our shops. Their citizenship is the same as those of us born in the country, their rights and duties the same as ours. It is very natural, therefore, to think that the various religions they espouse are much the same too. Are they not merely different ways of understanding the same God?

This is a very attractive idea. Far too many disagreements, persecutions and wars have arisen because of religious differences. So let's assume there is one God whom the different religions are all seeking in their particular ways. Let the Muslims and the Christians, the Hindus and the Buddhists agree that they are worshiping the same God, albeit in different ways, and leave it at that! After all, that must be the common-sense view, and it is also the tolerant view – and tolerance is a very attractive virtue, especially these days when traditional morals are widely discounted. Moreover, most of the great religions have a lot of ethical convictions in common: they are often peace-loving and kind, and none of them advocate murder, rape or theft. So why not take the views of the various different religions and build up a composite picture of God? Surely that would further world peace and understanding?

Not only is this the common-sense view, but it is backed up by some very significant thinkers. For instance, the saintly Indian leader Mahatma Gandhi said, "The soul of religion is one, but it is encased in a multitude of forms." The Hindu mystic Ramakrishna used to speak of himself as the same soul that had been born previously as Rama, Krishna, Buddha and Jesus.

Such a view is very old: the Roman Emperor Septimius Severus hedged his bets by having in his private chapel not only the statues of deified emperors, but those of the miracle worker Apollonius of Tyana, Abraham, Orpheus and Jesus Christ. What is more, this view is also highly contemporary. Not long ago the pop group Quintessence were singing this song:

> Jesus, Buddha, Moses, Gauranga,
> Draw me deep in the sea of your love.
> Jesus, Buddha, Moses, Gauranga,
> Oh maya, oh maya, oh maya.

This sort of syncretism is very attractive, but it will not do. Why not?

First, because if you ask the actual worshipers within different faiths whether all religions are the same, you will get an emphatic denial. They know very well that Christians are different from Muslims and Hindus, and often they are so persuaded of the rightness of their own religion that they slaughter members of other religions and burn their mosques or churches. It is, for example, written in the Qur'an, "Fight and slay the pagans wherever you find them" (Qur'an, sura 9.5), and in Nigeria and the Sudan this is happening on a widespread scale as I write. It is the academics sitting in their studies who write books saying that all religions are the same: the practitioners on the ground think differently.

Moreover, even the most cursory examination of the world religions will show that there is no way they can all be explained as the same. For one thing, they hold diametrically opposing views of what God is like. The divine in Hinduism is impersonal, though approached through countless deities and statues. The Muslim Allah is personal, with no subordinate deities and an absolute prohibition of idols or any other way of representing God. Buddhism is religion without God, and without even a final existence. Christianity teaches that God both forgives a person and also offers supernatural aid. In Buddhism and Hinduism there is no forgiveness, only ruthless karma, and no supernatural aid.

And what, according to the different religions, is the goal of our lives? Where are we heading after this life on earth? The goal of all existence in Buddhism is *nirvana*, extinction or "the complete cessation of both desire and personality" – attained by the Buddha after no less than 547 births. Muslims look forward to a sensual paradise with wine, women and song. The goal of all existence in Christianity is to know God and enjoy Him forever in the company of His redeemed people. So, what the religions teach differs enormously.

Even those religions that believe in a personal God do not agree on if and how He shows Himself to us. Islam denies that Allah ever reveals himself in person to humankind: he reveals only his will, and the proper reaction to that is *islam*, which does not mean as is often suggested "peace", but rather "submission". Christianity declares that God reveals not only His will but His person: indeed, He came to show us what He is like in the only terms we could fully understand, the terms of a human life: that is what Christmas celebrates.

Perhaps the greatest difference of all lies in the Christian assertion that none of us can save ourselves and make ourselves acceptable to God, try as we may: while almost all the other faiths assert that by keeping their teachings a person will be saved, fulfilled or reborn. I know of nothing that spells out this contrast more powerfully than the Buddhist story which starts off so like the parable of the Prodigal Son. The spendthrift boy comes home and is met by the father, and then has to work off the penalty for his past misdeeds by years of servitude to his father. How different from the unbounded love of the father in the Gospel story who does not dream of making the lad one of his servants but lays on a great feast to welcome him home. The principle of *karma* (cause and effect, paying off your guilt) is poles apart from *grace* (free forgiveness when you don't deserve it a bit). Indeed, the basic worldview of the Judeo-Christian faith, that a loving personal God longs to have relationship with His creatures, is in irreconcilable contrast with the view of Eastern religions that there is no personal God at all and that the best we can hope for is extinction and absorption into the sea of undifferentiated being.

These are only a handful of the differences that separate the entire world views of the great religions. Many people who say, "All religions are much the same" have never thought deeply about it at all and are quite ignorant of the differences outlined above. But how can any serious thinking person still make that claim? Their response is very subtle. They recognize that there are all these irreconcilable differences between the different religions but maintain that there is a "God behind God" where all differences are reconciled. In that sense, they say, all religions are the same.

That view has never been better put than in the old Hindu story of the king and the elephant. A number of blind men were asked to describe what they felt when they were introduced to different parts of an elephant. One felt its trunk and said, "a palm tree", another felt its tail and said "a rope" and so on. They all had different explanations but failed to realize that it was the same elephant they were all experiencing. They were blind, but the wise king could see the truth that all were touching the same elephant.

Now this story is often used in liberal literature on the subject to show that all religions are the same. But so often these writers fail to recognize the arrogance of their claim. For what they are in effect maintaining is that they are like the wise king who can see that all religions are the same, while the worshipers remain blind to the fact. We are entitled to ask, "Who gave these people such privileged insight?", "What reason is there to suppose they are right?", and "Why on earth should we imagine that they (when some of them are atheists!) know better than the actual worshipers?"

One could mount an even stronger attack on the idea that "all religions are basically the same, at least in their essential nature, even if their non-essentials differ so widely." If that were so, how would we be able to distinguish the essence of a religion from its supposed non-essentials? What principle could we use? Presumably we would make our judgment on the grounds that some elements in a religion are better than others. But from what vantage point shall we decide which is better? And does not the whole question of truth get bypassed and swept under the carpet by throwing them all into a saucepan, boiling them up, and straining off the essence? What if one religion really does give a fuller expression of that essence than another? And what if the Absolute really has come into our midst, and God Almighty has actually visited His people? If that were found to be the case, what would we be bound to make of the many examples of the relative, the other faiths? One thing is certain. We could emphatically not claim that they were all the same thing.

Christianity stands out from all other faiths. It maintains that the living God has come to share our human situation, died an agonizing death in which He took responsibility for human wickedness and broke the last barrier, death, on the first Easter day, with incalculable consequences for His followers and the whole world. No other faith claims anything like that. Christianity may be wrong, but nobody with his head screwed on can claim that it is just the same as other religions. No, whether we like it or not, we have to admit that all religions are not the same.

Chapter 3

"But Surely All Religions Lead to God?"

Do they? Who says? Think about it for a moment.

I assume you mean by "religion" some sort of fellowship or intimacy with the divine. OK? Well, many religions have no such aim! You see, there are not only different religions, but quite different types of religion, with very different objectives. Here are some.

First, there are *occult* religions, such as animism, witchcraft, magic and some elements of the New Age. These are concerned with spirits, often evil spirits, that need to be placated or manipulated. They may dwell in trees, sacred sites or people. They may belong to the ancestors or to nature. These spirits are as varied as the African witch doctor, the Mongolian shaman and the local sorcerer who seek to manipulate them. Occult religions are about spirits, not about God, let alone intimacy with Him.

Second, there are what you might call *imperial* religions. They are not about God either. They are about the highest political authority, which demands total allegiance – from the divine kings in Egypt and Mesopotamia, through the Caesars of the Roman empire, to the Shinto emperors of Japan – together with Hitler, Mao and Stalin in our own day. It is interesting to notice the "divine" notes struck both by Hitler and Stalin. Stalin used to have gigantic pictures of himself projected against low-lying clouds above mass rallies, while Hitler used messianic language about himself and predicted a Reich of a Thousand Years.

Third, there are *ascetic* religions, such as Jainism, Buddhism, some strands in Hinduism and all the "do it yourself" versions of Christianity. They are not about God either, but about self-renunciation. The self is renounced and mortified in order to diminish its grip and to rid the person of being tied to this world. Sometimes, as in Buddhism, it is supposed to lead, after many lives, to the final elimination of the self, which is absorbed into the impersonal One or Monad. It has nothing whatever to do with intimacy with God. Indeed, in most branches of these ascetic religions there is no God to be intimate with!

Fourth, there are what one can only call *genital* religions or fertility cults. They worship sex. This type of religion is very old, and very modern. It ranges from the fertility cults of the Canaanites, through the lascivious statues in many Hindu temples, through places like London's Soho and Amsterdam, to today's XXX films and videos and the astronomical sales of pornography. They too have nothing to do with God, let alone fellowship with Him.

Fifth, there are the *bourgeois* religions, which feed the religious instincts of the leisured classes and cost their adherents nothing apart from massive financial contributions. They are bodies like Christian Science, Spiritualism, Scientology, Theosophy and many of the self-improvement cults. They are all about man, not God and intimacy with Him.

Sixth, there are *prophetic* religions, which arise from the dynamic leadership and moral challenge of a great leader and tend to sweep across the world within a century of their origin. Islam, which made enormous inroads into the Middle East and North Africa within a few decades of the death of Muhammad, is one excellent example. Marxism is another. It profoundly influenced a third of the world within a few decades of Marx's death. Although it was militantly atheistic, Marxism had a passionately held creed, high ideals, self-sacrifice and clear convictions about the future in common with many religions. Its adherents would gladly die for it, as they would for Islam. But even Islam, despite its high view of God, does not offer the worshiper intimacy with God: "Allah reveals his message. He never reveals himself." The worshiper prays to him but cannot be said in any way to know Allah or have intimacy with him. Such a claim is deemed blasphemous. You can be killed for making it.

Finally, there are the *revelatory* religions. There have only been two (closely connected) religions in world history that teach that God can be personally known by the believer. Only Judaism and its "child" Christianity maintain that God has given a reliable and personal disclosure of Himself to humankind. Judaism tells of God's revelation of Himself through His mighty deeds of deliverance for Israel and through the words of the prophets. The Jewish people believed that God's only residence on earth was the space between the wings of the cherubim figures above the "mercy seat" of the ark: this was located first in the moveable tabernacle and then in the temple at Jerusalem. Of course, Judaism is very differently placed today. There is no ark, no priesthood, no sacrifices, no tabernacle, no temple. Modern Judaism is reduced to religious law, morality and synagogue worship.

The other faith that developed this strain of divine revelation, so strong in Judaism, is Christianity – or rather Jesus Christ. He claimed to be the fulfillment of all God's promises to Israel and to be the final revelation of God to humankind. He was Emmanuel, "God with us". *"In him,"* claimed the apostle Paul, *"the whole fullness of deity dwells in bodily form"* (Colossians 2:9). And so the Christian can say with the apostle Paul, *"I know whom I have believed"*, or with the apostle John, *"by this we know that he abides in us, by the Spirit which he has given us"* (2 Timothy 1:12; 1 John 3:24). Intimacy with God is what the Christian faith is all about. That cannot be claimed for any of the others.

It really is ludicrous to suppose that all religions lead to God, when Buddhism does not believe that there is any God at all, when Islam makes him so far removed, when Hinduism offers extinction after many incarnations and in the meantime sanctions idolatry on a massive scale. How can all religions lead to God when they have such different beliefs about God, the afterlife and how one can attain it?

Take, for example, the two views of history represented by Christianity and Hinduism. It is all the difference between the wheel and the road. The great emblem of Hinduism is the wheel, embodying the cycle of birth, growth, death and rebirth. It is always moving yet always turning upon itself. The wheel offers only one way of escape from this meaningless, endless movement. That is to take a spoke – it does not matter which one – and travel along it to the hub, where all is at rest and you can observe the ceaseless movement without being involved in it. They see this as a parable. It does not matter which religion you take: follow it to that timeless, motionless center where all is peace and where you can understand the endless move-ment which makes up human history – understand that it goes nowhere and means nothing. It is all an illusion.

The other great symbol is not a wheel but a road. That is the view of history taken by Christianity. It has a beginning in time, a midpoint (the coming, dying and rising of Jesus Christ) and a goal. That goal is not some timeless reality hidden behind all the variety and change of daily life. No, history is going somewhere. It has a purpose. And the goal for God's redeemed people is to enjoy intimate and un-interrupted communion with the Lord of history forever, in heaven.

Let me put it another way. There are two powerful reasons why all religions do not lead to God. The first is because of the nature of God. If there is a God at all, He must be the source both of humankind and our environment. The prophet asks:

> *"Have you not known? Have you not heard? Has it not been told you from the beginning? It is he who sits above the circle of the earth, and its inhabitants are like grasshoppers ... the nations are like a drop from a bucket, like dust on the scales."* (Isaiah 40:21, 22, 15)

That is the majestic God we are talking about. How can we possibly climb up to Him? It cannot be done. Far from all religions leading to God, *no* religion can lead to God. He is too great. The creature cannot possibly discover the Creator unless He chooses to disclose Himself. That is one reason why all religions are bound to disappoint. Do you know that little poem "If"?

> If
> all religions
> lead to God,
> how come
> most of them,
> having been given
> a thousand years at least,
> haven't yet
> arrived?

If by "religion" we mean humanity's search for the divine, it is bound to fail. What we need is not to compare the chinks of light that different religions may have perceived, but to experience the sunrise, which eclipses the light of every candle. We do not need a religion, but a revelation. And that is precisely what Christianity claims to be. Unlike other holy books, the Bible does not record the story of human beings in search of God, but of God in search of human beings.

There is a second reason why no religion will ever reach through to God. Not simply because of the nature of God, but because of the nature of human beings. The Bible gives a very unflattering picture of humankind, but one that is uncomfortably near the mark. It tells us, for instance, that we do not all have hearts of gold as we fondly suppose, but that the human heart is deceitful above all things and desperately wicked. It tells us that the murders and adulteries, the lies and folly do not proceed from our circumstances, but from our hearts. It tells us that there is no difference between us, for all have sinned and come short of God's glorious standard. It tells us that people love darkness rather than light because their deeds are evil (Jeremiah 17:9; Mark 7:20–23; Romans 3:23; John 3:19). There is something twisted in our nature (along with much that is good). As a result, we do not want God interfering in our lives. We want to paddle our own canoe. And even if we do engage in a serious search for God, there is the ball and chain of our own misdeeds hanging around our ankles. All of us fail to qualify, whether we come from the so-called Christian West, the Communist bloc, or the mystic East. None has arrived at God, both because He is too great for any of His creatures to pierce His incognito, and also because His creatures are too twisted, too self-centered to want to get near Him. The greatness of God and the sinfulness of human beings are the two massive reasons why all religions do not lead to God.

Many who urge that all religions do lead to God offer us the image of a mountain, with a number of routes going up to the top. It does not matter which route you take: any of them will get you to the top. We have seen that this view is untenable. I want to offer you a different analogy. What if the real situation is like people trying to find their way through a maze? There are lots of routes that bring us to a dead end and fail to get us out of the maze. There is just one way through.

That is the astounding and, at first sight, arrogant Christian claim, and we shall be examining it in the remainder of this little book.

These ideas, ie. are lazy thinking,
laziness.
It is pretentious sophisticated.
air-headed arrogance. The fury
who / says it puts his ignorance on display

Chapter 4

What Makes Jesus
So Special, Then?

Notice that I do not ask, "What makes Christianity so
special?" In many ways it is not special at all. If shares the
frailties and failures of other religions. Its history has been
marred by war and torture, lies and greed. As an institution
it shows the characteristics of many secular organizations.
Moreover it is frequently boring, moralistic and authoritar-
ian. This book is not intended to argue that Christianity is
better than other faiths. Christians are – and have been – as
fallible as anyone else. No. It is *Jesus* who is so special! I
make no bones about the fact that I am passionate about
Jesus. But this is not a blind and fatal attraction! There are
good reasons why I believe He is the way from God to us
and the way for us to God, and the following chapters will
show some of those reasons. But I do not expect the reader
to follow me – yet! I have hitherto given no reasons for my
allegiance to Jesus. So let us look at the question head on:
what makes Jesus so special? There are many great religious
geniuses. Why should anyone bother to give Jesus their
preference, and especially why should anyone be so infatu-
ated by Him that all the others are sidelined?

After all, there are many similarities between Jesus and
His teaching and that of other great men. Jesus, Buddha,

ı.Marx and Muhammad all lived in poverty, and were
2.rejected by the majority of their contemporaries. All
3.followed a great ideal. All suffered opposition and varying
4.degrees of persecution. All were passionately convinced of
5.the message they came to bring. All were very critical of the
religious situation around them. All advocated radical
moral change. All hoped for a corporate future for humankind that was much better than the present. Very well
then, what, if anything, marks Jesus out from the ruck of
religious teachers? What makes Him so special? Let me first
make three preliminary suggestions here, and then in the
chapters that follow we will look more closely at the four
main reasons for regarding Jesus Christ as unique and
supreme above all others.

First, the *influence* of Jesus was special. Nobody in all
history has had such an influence. Today, more than a third
of the world's population professes to follow Him, and no
faith has ever had so many worshipers as Christianity. In
1961 the Beatles claimed to be more famous than Jesus
Christ. But five years later George Harrison was singing "My
sweet Lord". The character of Jesus has dominated the
world in the two thousand years since He walked the hills
of Galilee. He is quite simply the greatest person who ever
lived. Napoleon had ample time to reflect on all this while
he was imprisoned on St. Helena, and he said,

"Alexander, Caesar, Charlemagne and myself have
founded great empires, but on what did those creations
of our genius rest? Upon force. But Jesus founded his
on love. This very day millions would die for him. I
have inspired multitudes with enthusiastic devotion:
they would die for me. But to do it, I had to be present
with the electric influence of my looks, my words, my
voice. When I saw men and spoke to them I lit up the
flame of devotion in their hearts. But Jesus Christ by
some mysterious influence, even through the lapse of

eighteen centuries, so draws the hearts of men towards him that thousands at a word would rush through fire and flood for him, not counting their lives dear to themselves."

To be sure, Muhammad has had a profound influence, but his lifestyle is scarcely comparable to that of Jesus. Muhammad's religion was militaristic from the earliest days at Medina. He raided passing caravans for their booty and exterminated the Jewish tribe of Banu Quraiza after the Battle of Khandaq in 627 AD. Although moderate Islamic countries may be peace-loving, Islam has often been, and in many parts of the world remains, the religion of force. That is very evident in countries like Nigeria and Indonesia. The Islamic attack on the Twin Towers of the World Trade Center is a current demonstration of the fact. Alas, some representatives of Christianity have been like that, but not its Founder. Jesus refused the way of force and embraced the way of love. The cross is the supreme example of that self-sacrificing love even for His enemies. But Jesus has also been the inspiration for courage, generosity, care for others, purity and any other virtue you care to think of. No wonder He has captivated the hearts and minds of peasant and king, of intellectual and illiterate all over the world and down the centuries. And today His cause is growing at about 100,000 a day (not a Sunday, a *day*!). We may not currently be seeing much of that in the West, but it is certainly the case in Africa, Asia and Latin America. It makes no difference whether you go to the Naga tribespeople in the hill country of India, the warlike Maasai in Kenya, the rainbow peoples of South Africa, the populations of Fiji and Finland, or Singapore and Sebastapol. Everywhere, and from every nation and culture, there are Christians and they are spreading. Often persecuted and reviled, they are not daunted. They have succumbed to the spell of Jesus.

You could have said something similar of Lenin or Mao. They had immense impact in certain parts of the world. Their followers have often gained improved living standards and found a goal to live for. But the appeal has generally been to one nationality or one class of person only. Mao and Lenin brought hope to the oppressed worker but offered nothing but doom to the bourgeois. Jesus too offers hope, justice and love to the poor, but His arms are spread out to all people, the rich and the disillusioned, the old and the young, the proud and the suicidal. He changes them all: but He does not threaten them or make them reject their culture. The influence of Mao and Lenin was based on ruthlessness, hate and a terrifying indifference to truth. Both of them were multiple murderers. What a contrast to Jesus! Where in the whole of human history do you find a character who has so dominated ethics, art and culture, medicine and education? Who has rivaled Jesus' appeal to men, women and children of every generation and type worldwide, and in so doing has transformed them for the better? Nobody has had an influence for good like Jesus of Nazareth. That's what makes Him so special.

Second, the *teaching* of Jesus was special. Nobody ever taught like Him. Such was the conclusion of the soldiers sent to arrest Him by priests who were jealous of His influence. He taught them, says the evangelist, as one who had authority and not like the religious teachers of the day (Matthew 7:29). His teaching was profound, lucid and memorable. Teachers before Him loved to quote authorities for their teachings. Not Jesus. He simply said, *"Truly, truly I say to you."* Who was this "I" who spoke with such power and attractiveness? Who else invited all and sundry into His Kingdom, and likened God to a great king who offered men and women a marvelous banquet, free of charge? Religious people who made excuses found themselves excluded, while the riff-raff of society discovered, to their amazement, that they were welcome. In what other faith do you hear of a God who throws a party and invites the utterly undeserving to come and enjoy it with Him? (Luke 14:15–24)

You have only to compare Jesus' teaching with the Old Testament to sense its power. Now don't get me wrong. Jesus took the Old Testament as His Bible. But He could still contrast His teaching with it, as fulfillment over against promise:

> *"Think not that I have come to abolish the law and the prophets; I have come not to abolish them but to fulfill them."*   (Matthew 5:17)

Read through the Sermon on the Mount (Matthew 5–7) and feel its power for yourself. The Old Testament had forbidden murder and adultery: Jesus goes deeper and forbids hatred and lust. The Old Testament had encouraged love for neighbor: Jesus goes deeper and encourages (and demonstrates!) love for enemies. The Old Testament had placed a limitation on revenge: *"an eye for an eye and a tooth for a tooth"* (and no more!). Jesus forbids retaliation altogether:

> *"But if any one strikes you on the right cheek, turn to him the other also; and if any one would sue you and take your coat, let him have your cloak as well."*
>   (Matthew 5:39–40)

Isn't that profound? But go further. Where can you find in the teaching of Jesus anything that strikes you as wrong? How do you account for the fact that there have been no moral advances on His teaching from that day to this? How did He get His matchless teaching without ever having been to college? How is it that it fits all people in every culture? What was the unrepeatable factor in His heredity and environment that produced such a remarkable teacher? Yes, the teaching of Jesus was very special indeed! If you could improve on it you would be on the front page of every major newspaper in the world.

Third, the *character* of Jesus was special. Never has there been a character like His, so humble and yet so strong, so prayerful and yet so down to earth, so peaceful and yet so energetic, so loving without sentimentality, so dynamic without being hearty. Nobody has been able to hold a candle to that matchless life, and nobody has been able to trash it either. Jesus is the only fully balanced person who ever lived. He had no strong points because He had no weak ones. He embodied all the virtues we associate with both men and women and none of the vices. In all the world He has had no equal.

Time and again He told the crowds not to follow Him unless His actions matched His words. And they did. Precisely. It is one thing to teach the universal love of God but quite another to lavish love on religious hypocrites, Roman soldiers, beggars and lepers – and on your disciples who betrayed you to death. It is one thing to say, *"Blessed are the poor"* and quite another to be happy while homeless and penniless. It is one thing to say, *"Bless your enemies"* and quite another to cry, *"Father, forgive them"* as cruel soldiers nail your bleeding body to a cross. But that is the way Jesus behaved. His conduct exactly matched His teaching.

That is something that has never been equaled. Socrates, Moses, Confucius, Buddha, Muhammad – or in our own day Mother Teresa, Martin Luther King and Billy Graham – all taught wonderful things, and people hung on their words. But never did any of these great figures actually manage to carry out all they taught. The Buddha had a pampered early life. Confucius's marriage was a disaster and ended in divorce. Socrates was unduly fond of young boys. Muhammad took eleven wives and numerous concubines (sura 33.50), although he claimed divine revelation for the maximum of four wives (sura 4.3)! Moreover he organized the murder of the poet Ka'b Ibn Al'Ashraf for writing sarcastic verses about him, and his head was cast at Muhammad's feet with the cry *"Allahu Akbar"*, "God is great", a cry that still accompanies many Islamic atrocities today. How different from the behavior of Jesus! Furthermore, all truly great individuals have had a consciousness of failure. That admission is actually one of the surest marks of greatness. But Jesus was different. He taught the highest standards that any teacher has ever formulated, and He kept them all. That is almost beyond belief, but the evidence for it is powerful.

His enemies could not make any mud stick on Him. Three times Pontius Pilate, who executed Jesus, declared Him innocent. Even the traitor Judas had to admit he had betrayed innocent blood. The brigands crucified with Jesus agreed that He had done nothing wrong, while the centurion in charge of the execution marveled and said, *"This man was innocent."*

If the evidence of His enemies is impressive, that of His friends is even more so. Normally nobody is a hero to His close friends. they know His weaknesses too well. But that was not the case with Jesus. One of the disciples, John, knew Him intimately and could call Jesus *"the true light that enlightens every man"* (John 1:9). He maintained,

> *"If we say we have no sin we deceive ourselves ... in him* [i.e. Jesus] *there is no sin."*   (1 John 1:8; 3:5)

Peter could call Him *"the righteous"* in contrast to us *"the unrighteous"* (1 Peter 3:18). Paul described Him as the One *"who knew no sin"* (2 Corinthians 5:21), and the writer to the Hebrews spoke of Him as the One we need, *"holy, blameless, unstained, separated from sinners"* (Hebrews 7:26). In short, every strand of the New Testament, written as it was by those who knew Jesus or knew Him well, is clear on the matter. Jesus lived a perfect life.

And that is what we may infer from Jesus' own words and behavior. We never read of Him needing to apologize or admit He was wrong. And that from the man who was so shrewd in spotting hypocrisy in others! In the Lord's Prayer He tells us to pray, *"Forgive us our trespasses"* but He never prayed like that Himself. Here is the man who dared to claim that He always did what pleased His Father in heaven (John 8:29). Here is the man who could turn to an angry crowd, angry because He claimed that He was one with God, and ask, *"Which of you convicts me of sin?"* (John 8:46) – and get no answer! Whatever way you look at it, His character and conduct were special.

These are some of the things that make Jesus special. I could make a big thing of them. But I choose not to. You see:

- Others have had great influence, though not so great.

- Others have taught great truths, though none so comprehensive.

- Others have lived fine lives, though none so fine.

In the chapters that follow I want to isolate four things that make Jesus stand out, not only as special but utterly unique.

Chapter 5

No Other Great Teacher
Even Claimed
to Bring God to Us

When the topic of conversation turns to God, people often give one or other of these responses: "Oh, you mean some great force behind the Big Bang – that brought the world into being? Yes perhaps, but He couldn't be bothered with the likes of you and me." Or else, "I believe this world is all there is. Call it God if you like."

The first group of people sees God as being so far away, so great, that He is unlikely to know or care about this bleeding world. The second sees God as so identified with this world of ours that we worship Him by worshiping the earth that mothers us. Both are reaching after something important. Any God worth worshiping must be unimaginably great and majestic on the one hand, and yet on the other so committed to our world that He really cares for each one of us.

And that is precisely what Jesus came to show. Enshrined in one of the New Testament letters there is an extremely revealing and ancient hymn about Jesus. It shows that Jesus came to embody both the greatness of God and His passionate and personal care for the likes of us. It claims:

"Christ Jesus, [who] though he was in the form of God, did not count equality with God a thing to be grasped, but emptied himself, taking the form of a servant, being born in the likeness of men. And being found in human form he humbled himself and became obedient unto death, even death on a cross. Therefore God has highly exalted him and bestowed on him the name which is above every name, that at the name of Jesus every knee should bow, in heaven and on earth and under the earth, and every tongue confess that Jesus Christ is Lord, to the glory of God the Father."

(Philippians 2:5b–11)

Those are among the oldest words in the New Testament, composed within twenty years of the death of Jesus. They embody a staggering claim. Think of what they are saying. First, that Jesus shared the very nature of God almighty. He was the only one in all history who actually chose to be born into this world. He humbled Himself by becoming one of us – and that must have been about as attractive as if we were to become a rat or a slug! The indescribably mighty Lord shrinks Himself to become a fertilized egg in a girl's womb. That, and no less, is the Christian claim. You must evaluate it carefully to see if you find it credible, but make no mistake: that, and nothing less, is the claim. Jesus is no witty rabbi, no wandering prophet, but God Almighty voluntarily limiting Himself to share our humanity in order, among other things, to show human beings what He is like and how much He loves them. In that coming to earth, that "incarnation" as Christians call it, you have the combination of a God who is incomprehensibly great and yet incredibly loving and involved with our situation. His love was willing to endure scorn, opposition and even death: worse, the cruelest death imaginable, death on a cross. Just why, we will see in the next chapter. For the moment, reflect on this claim made by one of His disciples:

"No one has ever seen God; the only Son, who is in the bosom of the Father, he has made him known."

(John 1:18)

In other words, if you want to know what God is like, take a long look at Jesus. *"In him,"* says another of His followers, *"the whole fullness of deity dwells bodily"* (Colossians 2:9). Peter, one of His closest friends, speaks of *"his divine power"* (2 Peter 1:3), and Jude, probably one of His own relations, speaks of *"the only God, our Savior through Jesus Christ our Lord"* (Jude 25). The writer to Hebrew Christians is very bold. He refers to Jesus as God's

"Son, whom he appointed the heir of all things, through whom also he created the world. He reflects the glory of God and bears the very stamp of his nature, upholding the universe by his word of power."   (Hebrews 1:2–3)

As you know, Jesus lived very simply and could have been mistaken as a mere wandering teacher. And yet He made the most momentous claims. He called God His *"Abba"*, an Aramaic word meaning ("dear Daddy". Nobody in all history is ever before recorded as having spoken of God like that. He claimed that He existed even before Abraham was born – Abraham who founded the Jewish race two thousand years earlier: *"before Abraham was, I am"* (John 8:58). He claimed that whoever had seen Him had actually seen God the Father (John 14:9). He claimed that He embodied resurrection from death and could give eternal life to those who entrusted themselves to Him (John 11:25f.). He claimed that nobody could know God as Father except through Him who made the Father known (Matthew 11:25–27; John 14:10–11). He maintained that at the end of time He would be given the task of judging humankind and separating the sheep from the goats, the saved from the lost (Matthew 7:24ff; 25:31–46).

Think for a moment what monumental claims these represent. Could anyone in His right mind make them unless He really did share the nature of God? Such a claim could never have crossed the mind of the Buddha or Confucius because they offered systems of ethical behavior, not fellowship with God. Muhammad was appalled by the idolatry around him in his early life, so the principal tenet of his creed is that Allah is one, and the principal sin is ascribing divinity to anyone else. Muhammad would never have dreamed of claiming to share in God's nature. If he heard anyone making it, it would have struck him as the most appalling blasphemy, and he would probably have had the heretic killed. Many of his followers have been doing the same ever since. As I write, news is coming in of more than 10,000 Christians murdered by Islamic extremists in the Central Sulawesi province of Indonesia and a further 8,000 forced at knifepoint to convert to Islam. But apostasy from Islam, *irtidad* is punishable by death. "If they turn back, then take them and kill them wherever you find them" (sura 4:89).

Any fair appraisal of the evidence shows that alone of the great teachers, Jesus Christ claimed to share the nature of God almighty while being at the same time a loving and humble member of the human race. This is utterly without parallel in any of the faiths of the world. It makes Jesus very special indeed.

Of course, it is one thing to claim to share God's nature. Quite another to so demonstrate it that hundreds of millions of people for the next two thousand years should be convinced about it. Yet that is what Jesus achieved. Let us be clear about one thing before we glance at the evidence. No Jew would readily tolerate the suggestion that God had come in person to this world. They were as passionately monotheistic as any Muslim. But all the first Christians were Jews: they had to overcome massive prejudice and skepticism if they were to recognize Jesus as the unique human being who brought God into our midst. And yet this is their consistent claim, as we have seen above. How come they were convinced? Let us recap a little and add to the points made in the previous chapter.

They were convinced by His *life*. It was matchless. Nobody could point to a single thing wrong with it, as we have already seen. For love, honesty, courage, self-sacrifice, sheer godliness – there has never been anyone to touch it. Gradually that had a massive impact on those living closest to Him, and made them wonder, "This life has none of the normal failings. Could Jesus be more than man?"

They were convinced by His *teaching*. It is the most direct, profound, authoritative, challenging and attractive teaching that human ears have ever heard. Read a Gospel, and see for yourself. The powerful and fascinating parables, the challenges to the religious leaders, the care for the poor and needy, the encouragement to the fearful, the teaching about human destiny, all make Him the most dynamic teacher ever. Compare the trenchancy of Jesus with the lengthy and meandering, though often beautiful teaching of the Qur'an, or if you have the endurance, with the Hindu *Bhagavad Gita*, or the 5,000 and more volumes of the Chinese Buddhist scriptures! Notice the contrast for yourself. The teaching of Jesus was so attractive that thousands of people went into voluntary unemployment for the privilege of listening to Him at length, and it was so direct and challenging to contemporary religion that it elicited the fierce hatred of the priests and led to His eventual execution. He claimed that His teaching was not His but belonged to His Father who sent Him (John 7:16). Increasingly those who heard Him came to the same conclusion.

They were convinced by His *miracles*. Nobody had ever done the things that Jesus did. There were miracles of healing: He healed the blind, the deaf, the crippled, and on occasion even raised the dead. There were the miracles over nature: the feeding of five thousand people with a few loaves and small fish, the changing of water into wine, the instantaneous quelling of a storm, and His walking on the water. In addition there were the miracles of His birth without a human father and His resurrection from the grave. These miracles are attested by Jewish and pagan sources as well as Christian. They were never done to show off or for selfish purposes. They were evoked by Jesus' compassion for human need. They were evidence that the long-awaited Kingdom of God had at last broken in. And they were visible signs of what Jesus offers to do for humankind. The One who fed the multitude can feed a hungry soul. The One who opened blind eyes can do the same for people blinded by pride and prejudice. The One who raised the dead can bring new life to someone who is spiritually and morally lifeless. We read that after one of His early miracles "his disciples believed in him" (John 2:11). The miracles were a powerful factor in convincing them that this Jesus was no mere man.

We shall deal with the cross of Jesus and His resurrection in two later chapters. These were of massive importance in convincing His followers that He was indeed God who had come to the rescue of humankind. But two other factors need a brief mention before this chapter closes.

People were convinced about His identity by His *fulfillment of prophecy*. The Old Testament was full of predictions about the day when God would personally intervene to rescue His people. They spoke of a king of David's stock whose dominion would be endless. They spoke of one like a Son of Man coming to God and receiving from Him a kingdom that would never be destroyed, together with power, glory and judgment. They spoke of a prophet like Moses arising whose teaching would be unparalleled. They spoke of a servant of the Lord whose suffering would be intense and whose death would carry away the sins of the people. They spoke of a Son of God whose character would measure up to that of His Father. This coming one would fulfill the role of prophet, priest and king forever. He would be born of David's line but in a humble, despised family. His birthplace would be Bethlehem. He would both restore Israel and be a light to the Gentiles. He would be rejected by His people, die among malefactors and be buried in a tomb supplied by a rich man. But that would not be the end of Him. He would live again, and the Lord's program would prosper in His hands. His death and resurrection would enable ordinary men and women to get right with God, whose Spirit would come and take up residence in their lives.

All this came true with Jesus. Not some of it: *all* of it. That helped to convince these orthodox Jews that God had indeed come among them in the person of Jesus Christ. For there is, of course, no other example anywhere in the world's literature of prophecies made centuries beforehand being subsequently fulfilled by a historical person. It was, and is, a powerful spur to belief.

The other thing that persuaded them that Jesus did indeed bring God to them was the claims He made. It is very strange. On the one hand, as you read the Gospels, you see in Jesus a humble, selfless figure, healing the sick, teaching the people, befriending the outcast. On the other hand, He makes the most fantastic claims, and many of them are casual, almost throw-away remarks. He takes it for granted that He is entitled to the worship due to God alone: when the disciple Thomas falls at His feet after the resurrection and cries, *"My Lord and my God!"* (John 20:28), Jesus accepts it quite naturally. No good man would do that. Clearly Jesus was more than a good man, or much less! Watch Him deal with a woman caught in the act of adultery or a paralyzed man brought to Him. In both cases He says, *"Your sins are forgiven"* and the paralyzed man demonstrated it by getting up and walking! What are we to make of a claim like that? The Pharisees knew very well what to make of it. *"Why does this man speak thus?"* they ask. *"Who can forgive sins but God alone?"* That is precisely the point. Jesus was laying implicit claim to do what God does, forgive human beings their sins (see John 8:1–11; Mark 2:1–12).

There are many other claims that Jesus makes: He claims to be the Bread of life without which people will go hungry, to be the Way to God, the Truth about God and the very Life of God (John 6:48; 14:6). He claims to be the Resurrection and the Way to eternal life (John 11:25). He claims to be the One who uniquely demonstrates God to us and brings us to God (Matthew 11:25–30; John 14:1–11). Read any of the Gospels – it will only take you an hour at most – and you will see many such claims. What are you going to make of them? There are only three options. Either He was crazy, or He was out to deceive, or His claims are true. Can you believe that such a person with such a quality of life and such marvelous teaching was mad? Can you believe that He who laid such emphasis on truth was an utter liar? If not, there is only one conclusion. This Jesus *did* bring God to us.

The atheist professor turned Christian, C. S. Lewis, puts it superbly:

"I am trying here to prevent you saying the really silly thing that people often say about him: 'I'm ready to accept Jesus as a great moral teacher, but I don't accept his claim to be God.' That's the one thing you must not say. A man who was merely a man and said the sort of things Jesus said would not be a great moral teacher. He'd either be a lunatic – on a level with the man who says he's a poached egg – or the Devil from Hell. You must make your choice. Either this was and is the Son of God: or else a madman: or something worse. You can shut him up for a fool: you can spit at him and kill him as a demon: or you can fall at his feet and call him Lord and God. But don't come to him with any of that patronizing nonsense about his being a great human teacher. He hasn't left that open to you. He didn't intend to."

Jesus is utterly unique in bringing God to us. Listen to Lewis again:

"There is no half-way house, and there is no parallel in other religions. If you had gone to Buddha and asked him, 'Are you the son of Bramah?' he would have said, 'My son, you are still in the vale of illusion.' If you had gone to Socrates and asked, 'Are you Zeus?' he would have laughed at you. If you had gone to Muhammad and asked, 'Are you Allah?' he would first have rent his clothes and then cut off your head."

Jesus is unique among religious leaders in claiming to bring God to our world in His own person and making good that claim by such powerful evidences.

Chapter 6

No Other Great Teacher
Dealt Radically with
Human Wickedness

It seems to me that the maturity and depth of any religion is best demonstrated by its attitude toward the evil, the suffering and the sheer wickedness that devastate human existence. Does God act with both justice and compassion? This is the area where superficiality in a religion is most obvious. It is also one of the areas where to imagine that all religions are broadly the same is laughably untrue.

Human wickedness has remained persistent throughout history, and it has its roots in every person who has ever been born. You only have to turn on the TV or open a newspaper, and it stares out at you: brutality, lust, greed, corruption, war, marital breakdown, rape, hatred, bitterness, oppression, indifference to the needs of others – and the rest. It is unfortunately an endemic part of human nature, and it remains intractable despite the goodwill of governments, the improvement of social conditions and the ministrations of psychologists, preachers and moralists. It just won't go away. It is the lasting proof that we do not have, as we fondly wish, hearts of gold.

Let us glance at what some of the world's religions offer us to counter the evil in human hearts and actions.

45

To emphasize the point that all religions emphatically do not have a common view on evil and suffering, let us begin with Satanism. Do not imagine that there is no such thing or that it is harmless. Deliberate dedication to evil, and indeed the worship of the devil, is widespread. It is not restricted to the Satanist Church, the Manson gang, or the box office smash *Rosemary's Baby*. Covens of black witchcraft are increasing all over Europe. Collateral interests such as involvement in the occult, astrology, fortune telling and necromancy are all on the increase. And none of them have any answer to the problem of human wickedness. They either encourage it or ignore it.

Confucianism, like humanism, is inclined to brush it aside. Confucius had a high moral code: indeed, Confucianism is more a fine ethical system designed to help people get along with one another than a faith designed to reconcile God and humanity. It is full of teaching about the way *Chun-tzu*, "man at his best", will behave. It contains the negative version of the Golden Rule: "Do not impose on others what you yourself do not desire" (*Analects* 15.24). Ah, but what happens when I fail to do this? Confucianism has no satisfactory answer.

Confucius taught that human nature is essentially good: as his follower Meng-tzu put it, "Though water naturally flows downward, it can be made to flow uphill but only as a result of external force. Likewise man's nature is basically good, but can be forced into bad ways through external pressure." This is a very shallow concept. To suppose that wrong words, deeds, thoughts and attitudes are solely the result of external pressures is profoundly unrealistic. How different is the analysis of good and evil given by Jesus:

> *"For from within, out of the heart of man, come evil thoughts, fornication, theft, murder, adultery, coveting, wickedness, deceit, licentiousness, envy, pride, foolishness.*

All these evil things come from within, and they defile a man." (Mark 7:21-23)

Buddhism does not help us either. It is more inclined to atheism even than Confucianism, but like that faith sets out to be a practical guide to life. In Buddhism there is no such thing as sin against a Supreme Being, for there is none. But there is a moral law of cause and effect. You inherit moral capital debt, so to speak, from previous lives, and you add to it (or reduce it) by your actions in this life. So the sum of your good deeds and bad deeds will reappear in another life. You have made your deposit into an account that will be drawn from in a reborn life. And so the depressing process goes on, for hundreds of lives, until and unless you manage to break out into enlightenment, like the Buddha himself. Thus Buddhism imposes endless rules for acquiring merit: 30 rules to curb greed, 75 rules for the novice seeking admission to become a monk, 227 rules for the male monk and 311 for the female! Here is a Rule Book to end all rule books! But it has no answer to human wickedness and no answer to suffering except through the cessation of all desire, and eventually the elimination of the self altogether.

Hinduism, from which Buddhism sprang, is somewhat similar except that it speaks of reincarnation rather than rebirth. Again there is no belief in a personal God but rather in Brahman, an impersonal ultimate reality. Again there is the same chilling doctrine of *karma*, the law of moral consequences. You pay for what you do. Not much hope in that, and not a lot of logic either. *Karma* demands payment for misdeeds – and yet there is no God to receive it!

Islam is far more realistic. It recognizes a Supreme Being, Allah. It recognizes that he is both compassionate and holy. It realizes that sin, human wickedness, has to be punished. And the Qur'an speaks a lot about judgment in the flames *as some writers say*

of hell. However, because Allah is unimaginably great and entirely separated from his creation, human beings cannot enjoy intimacy with him. Sin, accordingly, is not seen as breaking God's heart but as rebellion against his will. The Muslim operates under a legalistic system embracing five essentials: the creed, prayers, almsgiving, fasting and the pilgrimage to Mecca. Islam teaches that on Judgment Day Allah will put your good deeds in one side of the scale, and your bad deeds in the other (sura 23:102,103), and you may or may not find mercy: "Allah punishes whom he pleases and grants mercy to whom he pleases" (Qur'an, sura 2.284, cf. 3.129, 5.18). Accordingly no Muslim has any assurance that Allah, however compassionate, will accept him to the delights of paradise rather than condemn him to the flames of hell. Consequently in popular Islam there are constant efforts to gain assurance of forgiveness. In some places Muhammad is raised to semi-divine status: he will perhaps intercede for you with Allah. In others the *pir*, or holy man, may be enlisted as an intermediary on your behalf. In yet others the prayers of the faithful and their offerings after your death may ease your passage through the fires and gain you access to paradise. But nowhere is there any assurance of forgiveness.

The Christian understanding is, I submit, far more profound than any of these. No other great teacher dealt radically with human wickedness. But Jesus did. The Bible acknowledges, as we have seen, the endemic nature of sin in the human heart. It is like a pernicious weed that keeps popping up however hard you cut it back or dig it up. And the Christian gospel maintains what makes a lot of sense: namely that God, the personal and infinite Creator of the world and humankind, is heartbroken when His creatures reject Him and go their own way. And He must judge the evil actions to which this inner rebellion gives rise. No God who is good and honest, true and lovely, could possibly pretend that evil is a matter of indifference. He could never pat us on the head and say, "There, there, it does not matter!" Because it does matter. It offends against moral justice in the world. Think of Hitler or Stalin as obvious examples of mass murderers. Is God going to do nothing about that? No, He must deal with it if He is the moral ruler of the universe. But on the other hand, as Islam has rightly understood, God is compassionate, full of mercy and kindness. The Bible goes much further than Islam and asserts that God is not simply the compassionate one who may or may not have mercy as He pleases, but that He is also the great Lover who longs to have close intimacy with us. It dares to say that God is love! So inevitably there is a problem. The holiness and justice of God cannot pretend that evil does not matter. It must be dealt with. It is like cancer infecting, spreading, and fatal. It must be cut out.

What, then, is God to do? His holiness must judge evil. But His love goes out to the sinner. How could He be, as one New Testament letter puts it, both "just" and *"the one who justifies those who have faith in Jesus"* (Romans 3:26 NIV). That is the problem.

The answer is breathtaking in its profundity. In short, it is this. God almighty loved us so much that He set out to win our obstinate and self-centered hearts. So He chose a people, the Jews, on whom He lavished great pains to show them what He was like and how they should respond. He had to work hard to prepare them for the day when He would come in person to this world: we call that time the first Christmas. He embodied what it was to be truly human, Confucius's "man at his best"; and for those who had eyes to see, He was embodying at the same time what divinity was like. He was the man who was God. He lived in humility and absolute obedience to His Heavenly Father and willingly shared in the sufferings of His fellows. He was accounted illegitimate, was nearly murdered after His birth in a filthy stable, and became a refugee. He lived in a poor working-class home, then as a teacher He had no home, no educational privileges, no income. He suffered unjust opposition, unfair trial and undeserved death through the most painful form of execution, crucifixion. He drained the cup of human suffering to the dregs. Nobody can say to God, "You don't understand." He does understand, because He has been through it all. But suffering as a whole is rooted in sin as a whole. The world is out of joint. People do not behave as God intended, and suffering is the inevitable result. There is a link, though not a direct one, between human sin and human suffering. And the most wonderful aspect of the death of Jesus is not only that He shared our sufferings but that He took personal responsibility for the entire filth, the trash can loads if you like, of human wickedness. When you and I do something wrong, it affects and diminishes us. Usually it hurts other people. And always it creates a barrier between us and God. It is this barrier between a holy and loving God and ourselves that Christ's death upon the cross dealt with. The God-man willingly bore upon His shoulders all the guilt before God of a whole world that had gone wrong. His death dealt with the offenses of everyone who had ever lived, and of all that ever would live, until Judgment Day. He carried the lot.

> *"For Christ also died for sins once for all, the righteous for the unrighteous, that he might bring us to God."*
> (1 Peter 3:18)

So nobody can say that God has failed to deal justly with human wickedness: He has paid the penalty for it Himself. He has undergone its foul consequences. Because He was man, He has acted properly as our substitute and carried the load of human guilt. And because He was divine, that sacrifice of His is eternal in its effect. It never needs to be added to or repeated.

Christ offered for all time a single sacrifice for sins. So we have been sanctified through the offering of the body of Jesus Christ once for all (Hebrews 10:10, 12). That is the glorious claim of the New Testament. So you and I can justly be forgiven. God's love invites us to return home. God's undreamed-of sacrifice means we can be accepted without a slur on our character. And, of course, once we have responded to that astounding generosity, it begins to change our behavior. That is why once people genuinely commit their lives to Jesus Christ there is, not perfection, but substantial moral improvement. His love for us lights a fire of devotion in our hearts and we long to live upright loving lives for Him. *"We love,"* says the apostle, *"because he first loved us"* (1 John 4:19). So not only is human guilt before a holy God dealt with, but the recipients of His forgiveness begin to adopt a very different lifestyle, out of gratitude. No teacher, no guru in all history has been able to make an offer of complete forgiveness and an utterly new start like that. Jesus is the only one who has dealt radically with human wickedness by taking its filth upon Himself so that we might never have to bear it. That is why His followers love Him and worship Him. There is no parallel to that anywhere among the religions of the world. And no other religion can give a satisfactory answer to how it is possible for us to have intimacy with God. However loving they may imagine Him, He must also be just. And how can a just God overlook our offenses? The only possible way would be if in sheer love He determined to pay our debts Himself. The Hindu doctrine of karma says, "You sin, you pay." The cross of Christ shows God saying, "You sin, I pay." And that is utterly unique!

Chapter 7

No Other Great Teacher Broke
the Final Barrier – Death

On April 27, 1783, Lieutenant General Sir Eyre Coote, KB, Commander of the British Forces in India, died. I have seen and marveled at the vast monument celebrating his achievements, which concluded "but death interrupted his career of glory." It tends to do that! "The first two minutes of life are critical", declared the notice on the surgery wall. Underneath someone had added, "The last two are pretty dicey as well." As another joker put it, "The most dangerous thing in the world is living. There is a 100 percent mortality rate."

This is a somber thought. For most of the time we manage not to think about it, until perhaps we attend a friend's funeral or ourselves suffer a stroke. Then we wonder if there is life after death. The English philosopher Thomas Hobbes expressed our attitude well: "When I die, worms will devour my body and I will commit myself to the 'Great Perhaps.'"

People have been doing that since time immemorial. I shall never forget visiting Lebanon and seeing some of the oldest tombs in existence. The skeletons were buried in a highly suggestive position. Their knees were tucked up under their chins, and they were encased in an earthenware egg. In other words, the men and women of that far-off day cherished the hope that new life would break out of the "egg" of death. They dared to hope that when they were dead, they might somehow live again. I recall being fascinated, during a visit to Italy, by the ancient Romans' preoccupation with death. There are many mosaics dealing with death and the afterlife at Herculaneum and Pompeii, the Italian cities overwhelmed by the terrible eruption of Vesuvius in AD 79. There are pictures of skeletons with jugs in their hands, of skulls lurking behind the revelers at a feast and inscriptions such as, "Remember you must die". One of the most remarkable pictures is of a phoenix, the mythical bird that was supposed to come to life again after it had been burnt on the funeral pyre: underneath it the artist had written, "Phoenix, how lucky you are!"

What have the great religions to say about the ultimate barrier, death? On the whole, they do not handle it very satisfactorily.

Both Hinduism and Buddhism believe there is an after-life. But it is nothing to look forward to. In Hinduism your *atman*, your spirit, is reincarnated in another body and you start paying for the bad things you have done in a previous existence. Buddhism prefers the word "rebirth" to "reincarnation", believing that another consciousness which is saddled with your moral indebtedness emerges after your death. So *karma* has the last word in both religions, unless you are fortunate enough, after many lives, to find that the good you have done outweighs the bad, in which case there is hope of *nirvana*, where all consciousness ends and you return to the fundamental One or Monad that underlies and embraces everything in the universe. There is no eternal life and no "you" to enjoy it. It is simply the case of all rivers flowing into the sea, and appropriately your ashes may be sprinkled on the Ganges River and so flow into the ocean. Not something to exult about. It is interesting that in the West reincarnation is becoming a popular concept to toy with as hedonistic, wealthy people hope that they may be even more wealthy and happy in the next existence. But in the East where the doctrine originates, *karma* is a very heavy load and nobody looks on it with pleasure or hope.

At first sight Islam is much more positive. It is clear that there is life after death. The last day, or Day of Judgment, figures prominently in the Qur'an (see sura 75, 81.1–19, 82, 83.4–21, 84). The day and hour is a secret, but there are to be twenty-five signs of its approach. All people will then be raised. The books kept by the recording angels will be opened, and Allah will weigh each person's deeds in the scales (Qur'an, sura 23.102f.). Those who follow and obey Allah and Muhammad will cross a narrow bridge to the Islamic paradise, though some of them may fall off into a temporary, or indeed final, residence in hell. The "infidels", i.e. non-Muslims, and the wicked will be tormented in the fires of hell. The Islamic conception of paradise is very sensual and very macho. There is not much for the women. Men will recline on soft couches and rich carpets quaffing cups of drink handed them by *huris*, or maidens of paradise. "They are virgin-pure and undefiled, with big, lustrous eyes" (sura 88.8ff. and 56.8–38). "They are untouched by men or spirits" (*jinn*, sura 55.74). This emphasis on sensual rewards and horrific punishments is repeated time and again in the Qur'an. However faithful a Muslim you are, you cannot be confident of paradise. "Feeling safe from the wrath of Allah" is one of the seventeen major sins in Islam, but it is tempered with another major sin, "despairing of Allah's mercy". For there is a strong doctrine of *kismat* running through Islamic teaching, the concept of fate. Both good and evil proceed from Allah's will, and that will is despotic and inscrutable. Even the promise that "the blessed shall dwell in paradise" is balanced by the further words "unless Allah ordains otherwise" (Qur'an, sura 11.108). So one of the most common Muslim phrases is the fatalistic *Insh'allah*, "if it is Allah's will". It is surprising that this note of uncertainty has been revoked in recent pronouncements from some Islamic sources that those who killed themselves and thousands of others in smashing New York's Twin Towers, and the Palestinian suicide bombers who slaughter as many Israelis as they can when they blow themselves up, will be assured of an immediate translation to the delights of paradise. Who says? How can we be sure that the reward for murder is heaven? It can scarcely be taken for granted! Nor does it reflect well on the religion that promises it.

This Islamic view of salvation based on good works and on the inscrutable will of Allah is easily understood, even if not very comforting. But how can we know it is true? We have to take the word of the "infallible" Qur'an for it. Muhammad died at sixty-two and did nothing to validate his ideas about life after death. He remained very dead, and his tomb is with us to this day.

That is where the Christian message is so different. Jesus Christ offers eternal life to those who love and trust Him. There is little on offer by way of sensual delights, but rather the joy of being in intimate relation with the living God and His people forever. In the pictorial language of the book of Revelation we read,

> *" 'Behold, the dwelling of God is with men. He will dwell with them and they shall be his people, and God himself will be with them; he will wipe every tear from their eyes, and death shall be no more, neither shall there be mourning nor crying nor pain any more, for the former things have passed away.' And he who sat upon the throne said, 'Behold, I make all things new.' "*   (Revelation 21:3–5)

There is little attempt in the Bible to describe life after death. It is "being for ever with the Lord", "departing to be

with Christ, which is far better" and being "with Christ" –
the language of relationship (1 Thessalonians 4:17; Philippians 1:23). In strong contrast to the teachings of any other
faith, membership of heaven is not earned by our good
deeds, however virtuous. It is the gift of the sovereign Lord
to those who entrust their lives to Jesus Christ and seek to
obey Him. Naturally, there is no compulsion about it. God
will not have conscripts in His heaven. Those who stead-
fastly turn their backs on God and refuse His gift of eternal
life have only themselves to blame. If they choose what the
Bible calls *"eternal everlasting destruction and exclusion from
the presence of the Lord"* (2 Thessalonians 1:9), God will
reluctantly confirm their choice. But they will have to push
past the cross of Jesus Christ, which He has erected as a
powerful barrier to stop people going to hell. At all events,
in the last analysis we all must choose. And God gives us
what we have really set our hearts on. We each go "to our
own place".

Well, you may say, why believe that any more than the
Islamic view of heaven and hell? A fair question, to which
there is a powerful answer. It is one thing to promise, as
Jesus did on the night before His death.

> *"In my Father's house are many rooms; if it were not so,
> would I have told you that I go to prepare a place for you?
> ... I will come again and will take you to myself, that where
> I am you may be also."*   (John 14:2–3)

It is quite another matter to validate such a claim by rising
from death to a new and radiant life three days later. And
that is precisely what Jesus did. The evidence for it is very
strong. Alone of the great teachers of the world's religions,
Jesus Christ rose from the icy grip of death. The bones
of Buddha have been divided up and are enshrined in
several different countries. The bones of Muhammad lie
in Medina. But the bones of Jesus Christ are nowhere to be

seen and revered. His body, His whole being, was raised from the dust of death by God His heavenly Father. He is alive forevermore. His resurrection from the grave is what started the whole Christian movement.

Nobody should believe a claim like that without good evidence. And the evidence for the resurrection of Jesus is not just good: it is compelling. Here it is in a nutshell. I have gone into it in much greater detail in *The Empty Cross of Jesus* (Hodder, 1998).

First and foremost let us get it clear that Jesus really did die on the cross. Islam has got hold of the notion that He did not: most Muslims believe that Judas Iscariot died instead. Actually the Qur'an is self-contradictory on the subject, for we read, "Then Allah said 'O Jesus, I cause you to die and then exalt you to myself and purify you from their calumny'" (Qur'an, sura 3.55), and that at the time of His birth the infant Jesus is supposed to have said, "Peace on the day I was born, the day I die, and the day I am raised alive" (Qur'an, sura 19.33). But the view that has dominated Islamic teaching is found in the Qu'ran, sura 4.156f: "They killed him not, nor crucified him, but so it was made to appear to them ... For of a surety they killed him not. No, Allah raised him up unto himself." The idea that Jesus did not die on the cross, but that it was someone else or an apparition, is an early Christian heresy found in the *Acts of John* in the early third century. Was Muhammad acquainted with its Arabic translation? Both the Gnostics who produced it and the Muslims were convinced that it was impossible for God to suffer. Not of course that the Muslims believe Jesus was divine: to ascribe divinity to anyone but Allah is shirk, the unpardonable sin. But Islam finds it impossible to imagine that Allah could desert a prophet in the fulfillment of his mission and also that it would be contrary to his justice to allow the suffering of an innocent person on behalf of others. So the Muslims are in difficulty about Jesus. They regard Him as a prophet, but not as great a prophet as Muhammad. And yet they believe Jesus was raised to heaven without dying, which makes Him far superior to Muhammad who certainly did die.

The death of Jesus on the cross is certain. It was a very public Roman execution and is attested not only in all four Gospels and the rest of the New Testament, but also in Roman and Jewish sources of the time, such as Tacitus (*Annals* 15.44) and Josephus (*Antiquities* 18.3). Indeed the inscription "Jesus of Nazareth King of the Jews", written in three languages and nailed to His cross, has probably been preserved, and identified recently by Professor Carsten Thiede. The Romans were very thorough about their executions. There is no doubt that Jesus was crucified, and the evidence for it is contemporary compared with the unsubstantiated Qur'anic assertion that dates from the seventh century!

Very well, He was crucified, but was He really dead? Did He perhaps recover in the cool of the tomb, walk out and persuade His followers that He was risen from the dead? That is a really stupid suggestion, although those desperate to refute the resurrection have been driven to it now and again over the centuries. For one thing, there is no record of anyone ever surviving a Roman flogging and execution. Even if Jesus had pulled off this astonishing survival, He would have been too weak to push aside the massive stone sealing the tomb. And even if He had done that, how would such a bloodstained, wounded and bedraggled creature have been able to persuade His followers that He was the Lord of life and victor over death? If you want final evidence that Jesus was dead, you have it in the eyewitness account that in order to ensure He was already dead one of the soldiers pierced the side of Jesus with a spear and out came *"blood and water"* (John 19:34). The ancient writer could have had no idea of the medical significance of what he saw, but any doctor nowadays can tell you that the separation of dark clot from watery serum is one of the surest indications of death. This gives proof positive that Jesus was dead.

And all the early evidence assures us that despite the fact that Jesus was dead and buried, despite the fact that the tomb was sealed with a massive stone, despite the fact that there was a guard on the tomb, Jesus was raised from the dead on the first Easter Day, and the tomb was found to be empty.

Would His enemies have moved the body? Of course not. At last they had Him where they wanted Him. Could His friends have done it? No. They were utterly dispirited and ran away feeling they had followed a discredited leader who had been executed and dashed all their hopes. They certainly did not expect His coming to life again: every account in the Gospels shows their utter amazement and initial refusal to believe. They could not have penetrated the guard and entered the sealed tomb, and if through some astonishing means they had done even this, they would never have gone all over the world proclaiming His risen presence with such joy that people felt they might be drunk, and with such persistence that prison, torture and death could not stop them. You do not allow yourself to get killed for proclaiming a fraud!

All the accounts proclaim that the tomb was empty on Easter Day, and there are delightful supporting touches in the Gospels. Here is one of them. St John's account tells of Peter and John racing each other to the tomb once they had heard from the women that He was alive. When they got there and stooped to look in, they noticed something very strange about the linen bandages that had been entwined with precious spices (a Jewish way of burial) and wrapped around Jesus' body. They were lying wrapped up in their original shape – *but with no body inside*. The disciples also saw the turban that had been around His head *"not lying with the linen clothes, but rolled up in a place by itself"* – and they saw and believed (John 20:7). Why? Because it was

apparent to them that the body of Jesus had emerged from
the grave-clothes, just as a butterfly emerges from its
chrysalis: and the turban lay apart, just like the cap of the
chrysalis once the butterfly has emerged. The enemies of
Jesus would not have removed the body of Jesus. The
friends of Jesus could not. Nobody else was concerned.
The circumstantial evidence of the grave-clothes supports
it. Therefore we are driven to the conclusion that the tomb
was empty because God raised Jesus from its clutches.

But the empty tomb is not the only or even the most
important evidence that Jesus had conquered death. The
Christian Church was born because of the first Easter.
Originally Christianity had nothing whatever to differenti-
ate it from Judaism, except this conviction that Jesus was
God's ultimate deliverer who had been crucified and raised
from the dead. As Paul put it in Romans 1:4, Jesus was
proved to be God's Son by His resurrection from the dead.
And the Church, armed with this conviction, which must
have seemed so improbable to Jew and Gentile alike, swept
across the Mediterranean world, making converts wherever
it went. Today it embraces rather more than a third of the
human race.

The early Church had three characteristics. You found
them everywhere. You still do. A special day, Sunday. A
special initiation rite, baptism. And a special meal, the Holy
Communion. All three are inconceivable if the resurrection
is not true. Believers baptized people into a symbolic union
with Jesus in His death and resurrection. They ate the
sacred meal with exultation and joy at the presence of their
risen Lord. And they managed to change the day of rest
from Saturday (in honor of God completing His work of
creation) to Sunday (in honor of God raising Jesus from the
grave)! Baptism, the Lord's Supper and Sunday all validate
the resurrection of Jesus Christ. It is inconceivable that the
Christians would have invented any of them if it had not
taken place.

But we can go further. The Lord appeared after His resurrection to large numbers of people. St Paul, writing a mere twenty years after the event, reminds His readers at Corinth of the fundamental importance of the resurrection: their whole faith rests on it. And He tells how Jesus appeared to Peter, the man who had denied Him, then to the twelve disciples, who had run away, then to more than 500 of His followers, presumably in Galilee where most of His ministry had taken place. He appeared to His brother James, who had not believed in Him in the days of His ministry, and finally Paul lists himself, the man who had ruthlessly persecuted the infant Church. Put that lot together: in addition to the original women who found the tomb empty on Easter morning, you have appearances (in a variety of locations) to fishermen who had followed Him for three years, to a skeptical brother, to a fanatical Pharisaic opponent, and to five hundred ordinary people, most of whom were still alive when Paul wrote (1 Corinthians 15:1–11). Pretty powerful evidence, is it not? Nobody, in those early days, could gainsay it.

And perhaps the most compelling proof of all is the way the lives of those first disciples were utterly transformed by their companionship with Jesus after His resurrection. Peter was changed from a coward who denied His master when the crunch came, to a man of rock whom the Jewish Establishment could not cow by dint of threats, imprisonment or a death sentence. The twelve disciples were changed from defeatists into a powerful task force by the resurrection. The five hundred were transformed from a rabble into a church: theirs is one of the greatest "comeback" stories in world history. All the disciples, including Thomas (John 20:26–31), came from unbelief to ardent faith. James, Jesus' skeptical brother, was changed by the resurrection into a believer who subsequently led the Jerusalem church. What accounts for it? Simple: *"he appeared to James"*. And perhaps most amazing of all, is the transformation of Saul of Tarsus, the ruthless persecutor of the Church, into Paul, the most fearless apostle of them all. The reason? *"Last of all ... he appeared also to me"* (1 Corinthians 15:7, 8).

Jesus has appeared to me, too. I have not seen Him in bodily form, but I have experienced His power and presence ever since I put my trust in Him fifty-six years ago! I do not *think* Jesus is alive. I *know* He is. He guides me in my confusions, encourages me in my low times, strengthens me to overcome my temptations, gives me a joy and peace that I could never find elsewhere, a love for others that used to be notably absent, and a wonderful purpose to live for. I can say with the apostle Paul, *"I know whom I have believed"* (2 Timothy 1:12). Not just know about Him, but *know* Him. And that is the privilege of the many billions since that first Easter who have become Christians. They are all witnesses to the resurrection. That can be said of no other faith. Jesus is special, because He has broken the death barrier. And because He is alive we can know Him and enjoy Him now in this life and be confident that after death we shall be with Him, which is far better than any joys this earth can afford. Unlike any other leader, He not only promises us eternal life in His company, but validates that promise through His resurrection from the dead. And that Confucius, Muhammad, Socrates and the others could not do. It does make Jesus rather special, don't you think?

Chapter 8

No Other Great Teacher Offers to Live within His Followers

There is no point at which Christianity differs more radically from all other faiths in the globe than this. Its founder offers to come and live in the hearts and lives of His followers! Let us examine this apparently preposterous claim.

In many ways Jesus was very like other great religious and philosophical teachers. Socrates had a group of followers who went everywhere discussing the nature of truth with him. The Buddha had a similar group. So did Jesus. It was normal in the ancient world. That is how advanced teaching was imparted – by a Master to his disciples. Thus far there was nothing unusual about Jesus. The staggering difference began to emerge on the night before His death. He started to teach them, what they could then only dimly understand, about the Holy Spirit. These were His words:

> *"I will pray the Father and he will give you another Comforter, to be with you for ever, even the Spirit of truth, whom the world cannot receive because it neither sees him nor knows him, for he dwells with you and shall be in you. I will not leave you desolate: I will come to you."*
>
> (John 14:16–18)

What could Jesus mean? To whom could He be referring? Islam has a fascinating answer. It believes that Jesus, for whom the Qur'an has a high regard as a major prophet from Allah, was predicting the coming of Muhammad six centuries later. This interpretation is impossible. The "Comforter" was to be with the disciples forever and would live in them, and the world would not see, know or receive Him. That could not refer to Muhammad or any other person: any human being would be visible and capable of being known and welcomed but could certainly not live in anyone else.

No. Jesus was referring to the Holy Spirit, whom they already knew in a sense, for He was embodied in Jesus. Jesus had been a great guide, teacher and comforter to His followers, and He promises that after His death they will receive "another" as Comforter, the Spirit of truth whom the Father would give to them. There are several references to Him in the discourses of Jesus on this last night with the disciples, recorded in John 14–16. The Spirit would be a lasting gift to them; He would take them further into the truth of God, flood them with Jesus' own peace, bear witness to Jesus and enable the disciples to do the same. They even came to see that it was to their advantage that their beloved Jesus was taken away from them, for otherwise the Spirit would not have come to them.

However limited their understanding of His meaning, His disciples would have been able to pick up the general thrust of what Jesus had to say, from their knowledge of the Old Testament. Here the Spirit of God is in evidence from the very beginning. Genesis 1:2 speaks of the Spirit brooding over the waters of chaos and assisting in the creation of the world. As the Old Testament progresses, the role of the Spirit is made increasingly clear. It is the Spirit of God Himself that we are talking about, not some spiritual aspect of human beings. The Spirit of the Lord is not to be domesticated by humankind, but is "other" and mighty.

That Spirit comes upon a craftsman like Bezalel, and as a result he does wonderful craftsmanship (Exodus 31:2–5). The Spirit comes upon an ordinary man like Gideon, and he becomes a mighty deliverer of his people (Judges 6ff.). The Spirit comes upon Samson and makes him the strongest man in the world (Judges 13ff.). But supremely we find that the Spirit of God inspires the prophets and enables them to speak God's words to the people of Israel.

There were, however, three great handicaps about the Holy Spirit in the Old Testament. First, the Spirit is seen as naked power: not personal at all. Second, the Spirit is not for every Tom, Dick and Harry, but for special people chosen by God, like kings and prophets. And third, there is nothing necessarily permanent about endowment with the Spirit in Old Testament days. The Spirit could be removed from a person if he or she were disobedient, like King Saul or Samson.

Those were the disadvantages, but the hopes were bright, especially in the writings of Ezekiel and Jeremiah. They looked for one who would spring from the royal Davidic stock, although it almost seemed to have been extinguished by exile, failure and death.

> *"There shall come forth a shoot from the stump of Jesse, and a branch shall grow out of his roots. And the Spirit of the Lord shall rest upon him, the Spirit of wisdom and understanding, the Spirit of counsel and might, the spirit of knowledge and the fear of the Lord."*   (Isaiah 11:1–2)

They also looked for the day when the Spirit of God would be generally available for all His people. This would come with the new and lasting agreement between God and humankind. Ezekiel had prophesied six hundred years before Jesus:

> *"I will sprinkle clean water upon you, and you shall be clean from all your uncleannesses, and from all your idols I will*

cleanse you. A new heart will I give you, and a new spirit I will put within you; and I will take out of your flesh the heart of stone and give you a heart of flesh. And I will put my Spirit within you, and cause you to walk in my statutes and be careful to observe my ordinances . . . and you shall be my people and I will be your God."   (Ezekiel 36:25ff)

Jeremiah, who lived at the same time, had a similar message:

"this is the covenant which I will make with the house of Israel after those days, says the Lord. I will put my law within them, and I will write it upon their hearts: and I will be their God and they shall be my people. And no longer shall each man teach his neighbor and each his brother saying, 'Know the Lord,' for they shall all know me, from the least of them to the greatest, says the Lord; for I will forgive their iniquity and I will remember their sin no more."   (Jeremiah 31:33–34)

This is mind-boggling stuff. God's people would all receive His Spirit. Instead of having God's commandments standing over against them in tablets of stone, they would have His commandments internalized within them by the Holy Spirit. Instead of just the top people knowing the Lord, they would all know Him. And instead of the sacrificial system, by which sin was brought to mind each year but not forgiven, their sins would all be completely and finally forgiven! A fantastic promise. Personal relationship with God, real forgiveness, and God's Spirit living within them to direct them in their moral decision-making so that they would really begin to please the Lord.

That is the background behind Jesus' promise to His disciples on that night before His arrest. He had Himself fulfilled Isaiah's longing. He was a descendent of David, a shoot out of the royal tree. And all the evangelists speak of the Spirit of God coming upon Him at His baptism in the Jordan and resting upon Him (as a permanent gift) throughout His ministry, so that His teaching, His miracles and His exorcisms were all the work of the indwelling Spirit. And now at supper, Jesus says to His downcast disciples, who were heartbroken because they knew He was to die, that the great days anticipated by the prophets Jeremiah and Ezekiel were coming good. His death and resurrection would release the Spirit of God that so filled Jesus Himself, into the lives of all His followers. And the Spirit would no longer be sub-personal, but marked forever with the character of Jesus. The Spirit would no longer be experienced as naked power but as a person: no longer an "it" but a "he"! And the Spirit would no longer be available merely for the chosen few but for all believers. He would universalize the presence of Jesus to those who had never seen Him or might live centuries later, so that they too could know and enjoy Him, just as those contemporaries of His had done. And perhaps best of all, there would be no danger of the Spirit being here today and removed tomorrow: He would be the lasting possession of the believer, the pledge of forgiveness, power, and knowledge of God.

I do not suppose the disciples understood all of this in the Upper Room on the night of the Last Supper. But soon it became a glorious reality to them. As we saw in the last chapter, Jesus was raised from the dead on the first Easter Day and before long returned to His Father in heaven, His work on earth done. His last act on earth was to reiterate His promise that the Spirit would come to them and would empower them to proclaim the gospel worldwide:

> *"you shall receive power when the Holy Spirit has come upon you; and you shall be my witnesses in Jerusalem, in all Judea and Samaria and to the end of the earth."*
>
> (Acts 1:8)

Jesus clearly identified the Spirit with Himself, spiritually experienced, for His parting words included these: *"lo, I am with you always, to the close of the age"* (Matthew 28:20).

What that amounts to is this. The Jesus to whom the prophet Isaiah had pointed forward was indeed filled with God's Holy Spirit. And now He promises the presence of that same Holy Spirit to be with the disciples in their own lives, after He had gone. The Spirit would make Jesus real to them and enable them to know Him personally, experience His daily forgiveness, and find His power for their mission of world evangelization. What was promised in the Old Testament had come to glorious fulfillment. And the disciples were thrilled with the reality they experienced. *"Christ in you, the hope of glory"* exults the apostle Paul (Colossians 1:27). *"Any one who does not have the Spirit of Christ, does not belong to him"* (Romans 8:9). There is much in the New Testament in that vein. Do you see what it is saying? That the secret of being a Christian at all is to have welcomed the Spirit of Jesus Christ into heart and life. It is not just trying to follow excellent teaching, as in the case of other religions, but of welcoming the indwelling Christ! How different from any other faith the world has ever seen. The whole infant Church was overwhelmed with this privilege. It rapidly became the community of the Holy Spirit, and the Acts of the Apostles tells the story of their reception of the Spirit on the Day of Pentecost and their subsequent dynamic outreach, all over the ancient world.

In particular the Holy Spirit living within them made a massive difference in the area of morality and lifestyle. Remember Jeremiah's promise that the law of God would be internalized within the believer? Well, it began to happen. Instead of the *"anger, wrath, malice, slander, and foul talk"* that belonged to their pre-Christian days (as Paul frankly reminds them), his Colossian readers have put on, like a wonderful clean garment, the new nature of the indwelling Christ. No longer is there any prejudice among them, based on race, class or religion. Christ is everything to them, and in all they do. So as God's holy (or separate) ones they *"put on . . . compassion, kindness, lowliness, meekness and patience, forbearing one another and, if anyone has a complaint against another, forgiving each other."* "Forgive," he says, "as the Lord has forgiven you." Above all else they must put on love, and must allow the peace of Christ to rule in their hearts. That is what they have been called for. And they must show their gratitude to God. They must let the word of Christ dwell in them richly. They must teach and admonish one another in all wisdom, singing psalms and hymns and spiritual songs, with thankfulness in their hearts to God. And whatever they do in word or deed, they must do everything in the name of the Lord Jesus, giving thanks to God the Father through Him (Colossians 3:12–17).

What a wonderful transformation Paul anticipates – even in these Colossian Christians he had never met. That is the quality of life that amazed the ancient world and enabled the new faith of Christianity to have such an immense impact. They set out to follow the example of Jesus and to please Him in everything. They did it in the strength that the Holy Spirit gave them. It was as if Jesus was living out His life afresh through them. That was and remains the heart of Christian morality. Not keeping a rule book, but loving and pleasing a person, and in His power overcoming the base tendencies of human nature and pouring out the love of Christ to others.

Behind the ethical teaching of the New Testament you keep sensing the example of Christ and His empowering. Listen to the apostle Paul, writing from prison,

> *"I have learned, in whatever state I am, to be content. I know how to be abased and I know how to abound. In any and all circumstances I have learned the secret of facing*

plenty and hunger, abundance and want. I can do all things through him who strengthens me!" (Philippians 4:11–13)

He can face anything because of the power of the living Christ within him.

That is a truly remarkable contrast to the ethical system of any other faith.

Christians did not operate like Buddhism, with its rule book or like Islam, with its fixed series of prohibitions, *haram*. They had no rule book, no *shariah* law, which calls for stoning for adultery and amputation of the hand for theft. Instead they sought to follow the example of the only perfect person who had ever existed, Jesus Christ, and in the power of His Spirit to approximate towards it. That is why they did not allow four wives and numerous concubines, as Muhammad would later do. Jesus had shown them the importance of one man one wife, as God had planned at the very start (Genesis 2:24). That is why they did not seek to further their cause by arms, like militant Islam, currently persecuting Christians in 32 countries: Jesus refused to take up the sword and so did His followers. That is why they did not kill apostates, as Muhammad later taught and as is still the rule in some Islamic countries, such as Saudi Arabia, Iran and Sudan. Jesus would not harm even Judas who betrayed Him. That is why they did not categorize people into orders of precedence or castes, like Hinduism, with a vast array of slaves and *Dalit* (untouchables) at the bottom. Jesus treated all people with equal love and respect. Christian morals were and remain modeled on the example and character of Jesus. They are not legal regulations, but an attempt to please the One we love. Progressively the Holy Spirit empowers us to do just that, if we rely on Him.

Often, alas, Christians fail to rely on the Spirit and His strength, and gross moral failures result. But these are not written into the Christian revelation as slaughter of

unbelievers and the inferiority of women to men are
written in the Qur'an (sura 9.5, 73 and 4.4, 34), where we
read, "Men have authority over women because God has
made the one superior to the other". The *shariah* (religious
Law) gives women only half the value of men in terms of
testimony and compensation. When Christians err, they do
not find injunctions to do it in the New Testament. Instead,
their wrongdoing results from their failure to follow the
example of Jesus and be directed by His Scriptures. The
great goal of Christian ethics, and the supreme work of the
Spirit of Jesus within us, is to make the believer like His
Lord. He intends us to be transformed from one degree of
glory (i.e. Christlikeness) to another by the Lord, the Spirit
(2 Corinthians 3:18). Our life is meant to be dominated by
love. When Paul says in that marvelous hymn to love in
1 Corinthians 13:

> *"Love is patient and kind; love is not jealous or boastful; it
> is not arrogant or rude. Love does not insist on its own way;
> it is not irritable or resentful; it does not rejoice at wrong,
> but rejoices in the right."*   (vv. 4–6)

he is sketching an ideal for the believer. But you understand
the challenge of that wonderful ethic only when you
substitute the name "Jesus" for "Love". Alas, Michael
Green is not always patient or kind. He is often jealous
and boastful. But Jesus is not. Jesus is never irritable or
resentful, arrogant or rude. And increasingly by the power
of His presence within us, Jesus works upon Christian
believers so that we begin to express His character. It takes
time, just as it took Michelangelo time to transform a block
of rough marble into a lovely statue like "David". But the
Christ who lives within keeps chipping away at us to
produce a similar result. There is only one teacher in the
world who offers to do that by taking up residence inside
disciples. His name is Jesus.

Chapter 9

Let's Face Some Hard Questions

Let us summarize where we have been so far. We have seen that it is ludicrous to claim that it does not matter what you believe as long as you are sincere. Clearly your actions on any topic spring from what you believe about it. It is equally foolish to imagine that all religions are the same. They are manifestly different in their conception of God, humanity, salvation and the life to come. Nor is it more intelligent to claim that all religions lead to God. For one thing the religions mean widely different things by "God", and for another they have widely different ideas of how to reach God. So we began to look at what makes Jesus Christ so special. Fundamentally it is because whereas religions in general attempt to find ways for human beings to reach God, Christianity at its purest maintains that it cannot be done, but that God in His generosity has reached down to us men and women in the person of Jesus Christ. In a word, Christianity is not a religion at all, but a revelation and a rescue and an ensuing relationship with God through Jesus Christ.

We then examined what made Jesus so special compared with other major religious leaders. And we found that He alone brought God into our arena. He alone dealt radically with human wickedness. He alone broke the barrier of death, and He alone of all religious leaders offers to come

and live within the hearts and lives of believers, so that
He provides not only an example to follow but also the
power to do so, as He lives out something of His own life
through us.

At this point a number of questions may arise in our
minds.

First, *is there any sense in which all religions have a common
core?* Yes, there is. Almost all religions believe in a superior
being whom we may conveniently call God. Almost all
religions believe in basic morality – few of them encourage
murder, adultery or cruelty, though a few, like the Sawi
tribespeople before their conversion, glorified murder and
treachery. And all religions lift people's eyes from their own
selfish concerns to some greater ideal. But that is about all
that can be said for what they have in common. In every
other respect they are extraordinarily divergent, as we have
seen.

Second, if the Christian account is true, *how should
Christians behave towards those of other faiths?* In the past
there have been terrible failures at this point. Christians
have at times behaved abominably to Jews and to Muslims,
and also on occasion to Hindus, notably while Britain was
in control of India. But of course cruelty and barbarity are
far from the attitude of Jesus and therefore should be far
from His followers. Jesus taught love to all. He taught
that we should go the second mile to serve other people
who do not think as we do. He taught us to bless those
who persecute us and do good to those who wrong us. If
Christians are true to their calling they should show the
same quality of love towards other people (be they atheists,
secularists or members of another faith) that God in His
grace and patience has shown them. That is the bottom
line. Anything less is failure and sin.

Moreover there are many ways in which Christians
and people of other faiths can combine on matters of
peacekeeping and justice, morality and social care in the

community, and do so with mutual respect and partnership. This demands no compromise in the religious views of any of the participants.

Another and even more sensitive question arises: *How should Christians regard other religions?* There have been three main attitudes among Christians to this question.

First, there are some who see other faiths as a preparation for the gospel. In the past Christians gladly learned from Greek philosophers and Roman poets and saw aspects in their teaching that pointed forward to Christ. Why should Christians today not learn more about community life under God from Jews, about devotion to God from Muslims or Hindus, about peacefulness and detachment from the passions from Buddhists, about the sacredness of life from animists, and about good ethics from humanists? After all, a Christian believes that all good, wherever it is found, comes ultimately from God. And so it is perfectly possible to have this positive evaluation of some aspects of other faiths while at the same time maintaining the New Testament emphasis that the full light has dawned in Christ alone and that salvation is in Christ alone, who died for those "who were far off" as well as for those "who were near".

However, another strand of Christian teaching tends to see all non-Christian religions as perilous. They are open to infection by spiritual forces that do not come from God, satanic influences that deceive people and lead them astray. This attitude is, perhaps, not as extreme as it sounds. Bishop Lesslie Newbigin, a lifelong missionary first in India and then in the West, who knew more about other religions than any other man alive, wrote a fascinating book, *The Finality of Christ*. In it he argues first that the demonic shows itself most of all in the area of religion (think of the religious wars current in the world today!), and he remarks on the care with which converts distance themselves from their inherited practices for that very reason. And second, he writes,

"It is precisely at points of highest ethical and spiritual achievement that the religions find themselves threatened by and therefore ranged against the gospel. It was the guardians of God's revelation who crucified the Son of God. It is the noblest among the Hindus who most emphatically reject the gospel. It is those who say 'We see' who most emphatically blot out the light."

A third Christian view of other faiths is to regard them not so much as preparations for the gospel or propaganda from the devil, but as aspirations of the human spirit. Buddhism, for example, is a noble aspiration of the human spirit to counteract suffering, while animism aims to appease the dread forces of evil spirits. There is obviously some truth in this, but it is inadequate because it does not do justice to the element of natural revelation in other faiths. God does indeed, as Paul put it to the Athenians intend that all people should *"feel after him and find him"*, for *"in him we live and move and have our being"* (Acts 17:27–28). He quotes with approval the heathen poet Aratus, "we are indeed his offspring". Moreover human conscience and morality are part of God's disclosure of Himself, for

> *"When Gentiles who have not the law* [of Moses] *do by nature what the law requires, they are a law to themselves, even though they do not have the law. They show that what the law requires is written on their hearts, while their conscience also bears witness and their conflicting thoughts accuse or perhaps excuse them . . . "*   (Romans 2:14–16)

So it would be misleading for Christians to regard other faiths as simply the record of human striving after God. Anyway, on the whole, we human beings are not honest seekers after God. We do our best to keep out of His way and are amazed (and threatened) when it dawns on us that in fact God is seeking after us!

It is probably best to regard non-Christian religions as a sort of patchwork quilt. They contain elements of truth that must come from God Himself. But there are also elements that are definitely false and probably come from the "father of lies", whose great aim is to keep humankind from the Savior. Moreover, other faiths undoubtedly contain elements of human aspiration after God.

But what is the situation of people who do not respond to the gospel? Here again there has been considerable divergence among Christians. Mercifully it is not up to us to judge: indeed Jesus expressly forbade it. *"Judge not, that you be not judged,"* He said (Matthew 7:1), and He reminded His hearers that judgment belongs to God, who will exercise it with full understanding of our circumstances and with great compassion. But bearing that warning in mind, Christians have tended to come up with three different views. All three, I think, are inadequate.

First, there is universalism, the view that everyone will be "saved" or brought into God's heaven whether they want it or not. While we would all like it to be true, the Bible flatly denies that idea, and it is utterly illogical. Would Hitler and Pol Pot feel at home in heaven? Is God going to stock His home with people who have no time for Him and no desire to live with Him for eternity? No. Jesus made it very plain that we have all been given the right to choose. And He made it equally clear that we must live with the choices we have made. So we read of sheep separated from goats on Judgment Day (Matthew 25:32–33), of the broad way that leads to destruction and the narrow way that leads to life (Matthew 7:13–14), of wheat that is gathered into God's barn and weeds that are burned (Matthew 13:24ff.). And so on. Always two paths, two destinations. Always a choice.

The second view envisages constant unending torment for all who are not Christians. There are many Christians who hold this view, but I doubt if it can be demonstrated from the Bible. To be sure, Scripture speaks about hell very directly, and nobody more directly than Jesus. He warns of *"hell where their worm does not die and the fire is not quenched"* (Mark 9:48), but that seems to be a metaphor from the city rubbish dump where there were always worms among the offal and where the fire was always smoldering. It was a picture of final destruction, not conscious unending torment. The language of "destruction" is the most common description of final loss in the Bible. We all have the choice: life in the age to come – or ruin for the age to come. There is indeed one passage in the New Testament that speaks about a lake of fire – but it is not prepared for people but for all principles of evil, which will be annihilated (Revelation 19:20). Christians should reject the idea of conscious unending torment as firmly as they reject universalism.

A third view found in some Christian circles is that non-Christians will be judged by God according to their deeds. But the whole Bible makes plain that nobody is saved because of their good deeds. For one thing those deeds can never be good enough for a holy God, and for another the whole idea of gaining relationship because of merit is disgusting. It is as if your child regularly washed the dishes and made the beds but never expressed love to you or even spoke to you. Would that satisfy your parental heart?

None of these flawed ideas matches up to the grandeur of the Christian gospel. In a nutshell it is this. Nobody deserves God's acceptance, but God in His great mercy has made provision for those who trust Him to be accepted through His sheer undeserved generosity. He has Himself carried away the burden of our badness by His self-giving on the cross, and so He is able with perfect justice to forgive us and declare us in the right with Him ... if we humbly ask Him for it. Wonderful! And those who do not respond to the gospel miss this glorious relationship with God, the very thing they were made for. Sadly, they miss it forever.

What about those who have never heard of Jesus? How will
they fare? Once again, we are in no position to judge. Jesus
has told us to leave all such judgments to God, who will be
utterly fair as well as passionately loving. But we have, I
think, an inkling of how God may operate. Think of all
those wonderful Old Testament believers, men like David
and Isaiah, Moses and Jeremiah. You have only to read
about their lives to see that these people had as intimate a
knowledge of God as we do. How come, if Jesus is so central
to it all? They had never heard of Him!

The great Christian theologian and apostle St. Paul had
clearly wrestled with this issue, and in Romans chapters 3
and 4 he gives us a brilliant answer. In His divine act of
reconciliation on the cross, God showed two things. One,
that He was absolutely just, so just that He could not
pretend that sin does not matter. But He also *"justifies him*
who has faith in Jesus" (Romans 3:26). And Paul goes on in
the subsequent verses to make it plain that the great men
and women of faith in the Old Testament were "justified"
in precisely that way. They were accepted simply and solely
because they put their whole trust in the Lord, as best they
knew how. They did not understand how He could accept
them, imperfect as they were. They simply trusted God to
find a way. And Paul came to see that the cross was
retrospective in its effectiveness as well as prospective for
those who lived after it. He came to see that God accepted
David and Abraham and people like that on the grounds of
what Christ *was going to do* in bearing the world's sin on the
cross. And God can accept you and me because of what
Christ *has done* for us on that cross. The only difference is
that we can see something more of how it was possible than
they could. That mighty death and resurrection of Jesus are
situated at the midpoint of time, so far as God is concerned.
Their shadow is cast both forward and back. So it may well
be that God will accept those who have never heard of Jesus
if they are like Abraham and David, who had never heard of

Jesus but trusted themselves entirely not to their religious views or virtues but to God's mercy alone. Such people may well be saved, not because of their religion, but because of what Christ has done for all. This view has much to commend it. It shows that God is consistent in how He treats humankind down the ages. It shows the seriousness of evil. It shows that we cannot save ourselves, but are perishing without a Savior. It shows that Jesus is the one and only Savior we sinners need, whatever our race and religion. It shows that God is scrupulously fair. At the same time it does not make the false assumption that people of other faiths are fine just as they are, that they do not need the gospel, or that they are saved by the profession of their own religion.

Does this possibility that there may be some people in heaven who have never heard about Jesus but have put their whole trust in God as best they knew how, enable Christians to sit back and do nothing? Does it cut the evangelistic nerve? Not at all. Why not? Because the very same apostle who cherished this door of hope was at the same time the most passionate evangelist who ever lived. He did not want to leave it to uncertain speculation, but longed to lead everyone he met from whatever faith to the Jesus who had transformed his life. Which leads us to the final question.

Should Christians try to convert members of other faiths? The answer must surely be "yes" for a number of reasons. In the first place it is the express command of Jesus Christ to go into all the world and make disciples (Matthew 28:19–20). Second, it is the natural thing to do: if you have found Jesus Christ to be rich treasure, of course you will want to share that treasure with others. Third, Christianity is essentially a missionary faith. It has been so from its earliest days. All the early Christians were converted from non-Christian religions (the converts had all been Jews or pagans). Furthermore genuine Christians have always felt themselves to be under an obligation to share the gospel with those who do not know it, just as you would be if you found a cure for cancer: you could not possibly keep it to yourself. So yes, evangelism is an essential part of Christianity. It has been well said that Christianity exists by mission as a fire exists by burning.

But having said that, it is vital that Christians behave with great courtesy to members of other faiths. They must pay them the respect of discovering what they believe and responding to that, rather than barging in like a bull in a china shop. They must affirm the good things in their religion – and there are usually many of them. They must live among them, love them and share their lives and interests: Jesus did just that! They must never hold out material inducements to faith, or they may produce the proverbial "rice Christians". And they must never threaten people and try to convert them by force. That route is forbidden to Christians. Jesus never forces anyone to follow Him. In love, He woos us all. And Christian evangelists must follow that pattern. Love, open discussion, bold proclamation and witness to what God has done in our lives are the fitting and indeed effective ways to pursue Christian evangelism in any culture.

Chapter 10

Where Do We Go from Here?

We have moved quite a long way in this short book. We have seen how empty are the commonly held ideas that all religions are the same, that it doesn't matter what you believe if only you are sincere, and that all religions inevitably lead to God. We have seen that real Christianity can hardly be classified as a religion at all. Religions are basically man-made systems to get through to and clock up merit with the divine. And they are all so different because human conceptions of the divine are so varied. But Christianity realizes this approach is never going to work. We cannot even begin to approach God until we know with confidence what He is like. And this is bound to be mere speculation unless and until He comes to reveal what He is like. The only faith in the world that claims He has done that is the Christian faith. It maintains, with good reason, that God has actually revealed not just His will (as in Islam) but *Himself* to us. Moreover He has made possible our rescue from our self-centeredness and blind rebellion by carrying the load of our guilt upon the cross of Calvary. Best of all, He is alive again and available to come and live by His Holy Spirit in the hearts and lives of those who will have Him. This will start a relationship that not even death can terminate. Such is the core of Christianity. As we have seen, it is not so much a religion as a revelation, a rescue and a relationship.

Inevitably, therefore, it poses us a question. If we agree that Jesus is so very special, because nobody else has revealed God to us, nobody else has dealt radically with human wickedness, nobody else has broken the death barrier and nobody else offers to come and enter the lives of those who invite Him – what is our response? What are we going to do about Jesus?

There are only three possibilities.

We may reject Jesus Christ. If we do this with full recognition of the issues involved and the consequences of our decision, that is a very serious matter. Of course we may always have the chance to change our mind. But on the other hand we may not. A heart attack or a train crash could extinguish our life in an instant. And then, presumably, we would go to a Christless eternity. I hope no readers will be so shortsighted as to say "No thanks" to the God who loved you and gave Himself for you. The outcome could be disastrous.

We may, on the other hand, defer a decision. In the ancient world some people, although persuaded of the truth of the gospel, put off doing anything about it until they sought baptism on their deathbed! Though not so spectacular, our attitude may be similar. "Yes, I can see the force of all this, but I don't want to do anything about it now. Too inconvenient to my plans, my pleasures, my priorities." Do you think that is a proper response to the one whom St. Paul called *"the Son of God, who loved me and gave himself for me"*? (Galatians 2:20). I heard once of a man in a railway carriage who was simply astonished at the care a soldier was lavishing on a man who could not coordinate his limbs, had several fits during the train journey, drooled at the mouth and so on. When asked why he should bother to give such affectionate care to his companion, the soldier replied, "This man was an officer in the Vietnam War. I was in his platoon. He saved my life when under intense fire, by risking his own. Enemy action reduced him to what you see now. I would do anything for him." Well, Jesus Christ did not risk His life for us. He gave it. And surely the only proper response is to say "yes" to the one who said "yes" to us, as the nails pierced His flesh. There is, of course, another reason why delay is unwise. The Bible encourages us to *"seek the Lord while he may be found, call upon him while he is near"* (Isaiah 55:6). And if you sense His nearness and turn your back upon Him, that makes it much more difficult to respond on a later occasion. Not impossible, but difficult, because you have hardened your heart.

Surely the wise thing and the grateful thing is to open up your whole being to the Savior. It is difficult to find language to describe such a momentous decision. The New Testament uses terminology like "believing in" Jesus, "repentance and faith", "coming to Him", and being incorporated "into Him". The point of all these expressions is that Jesus Christ and ourselves come into a living relationship. We connect up. It is God's initiative that brings us to that point, and all we do is respond. I love the story of the Prodigal Son (to which I referred earlier) who is so overwhelmed by his father's love that he asks to be taken on as a slave and finds he is honored with the best of everything and welcomed back as a beloved son (Luke 15:11–24). The idea of "coming home" is very moving, and accurate! I also love the story of the man in the Gospels who was asked if he believed Jesus could heal his desperately ill son. His reply, *"I believe; help my unbelief"* (Mark 9:24) seems to fit in so well with our uncertain age. But most of all I love the promise of Jesus Christ in Revelation 3:20. He says:

> *"Here I am! I stand at the door and knock. If anyone hears my voice and opens the door, I will come in..."*
>
> (NIV)

You may have seen a famous painting to illustrate that
promise, by the pre-Raphaelite artist Holman Hunt.
Curiously, he painted two originals, one hanging in Keble
College, Oxford and the other in St. Paul's Cathedral. It is a
picture that brilliantly brings out the meaning of Christ's
promise to us. It shows us a house with creepers growing up
the door, which itself has no handle. And outside stands
Jesus Christ, with a lantern in His hand (for He is the Light
of the world), robed in white with a red cloak to denote His
sinless life and sacrificial death, and this is underlined by
the crown of thorns on His head and the nail-pierced hand
that knocks on the door. The creepers up the door show He
has been waiting a long time. The absence of a handle on
the outside shows that the door has to be opened from the
inside. I suppose I love that promise and that picture
because they combined to bring me to trust Christ, many
years ago.

The point is very clear. That house represents our lives.
The Lord Jesus Christ, who stands excluded outside, both
made the house at our birth and bought it back, so to speak,
at great cost on the cross after we, the tenants, had stolen it
from Him. He made it: He bought it. It is doubly His. He
stands there as the holy One who cannot abide evil and as
the self-giving One who bore the agony of the cross for us.
He stands there patiently knocking. In my case He had been
doing it for years. How about you?

Why does He not enter? Because the tenant does not ask
Him. That is, I suppose the depth of human sin: not so
much to do terrible things, but to cultivate an attitude of
rejection that goes our own way and keeps Jesus Christ, the
most wonderful and loving person who has ever lived,
excluded from our lives.

But does He give up? No. He stands there knocking. His
promise is to enter the life of "anyone" who hears His voice
and "opens the door". It is obvious enough what He
means. Real Christianity consists in having the unseen

presence (or Holy Spirit as Christians call it) of Jesus Christ living in your very heart and life. Jesus offers to come in – if we will have Him. He does not only offer, He promises that if anyone (including you) opens the door He will come in. Not "may" come in: no "perhaps" about it. He *will* come in.

It seems a bizarre offer. *How can Christ who lived so long ago enter a human life?* By means of His living Holy Spirit. That is the best I can do by way of explanation. The rest is up to you. You can and will experience it, if you ask Him in.

But don't I have to clean up my act first and redecorate the house? No. He accepts us just as we are, and in the course of time He does the redecorating. If we could redecorate our lives by ourselves, He would not have needed to leave His home in heaven to rescue us!

"But I don't understand it all," you may well say. Neither do I. How can you understand love? You don't put it in a test tube and analyze it. You open your arms and welcome the lover. That is how Jesus invites you to respond to His love.

But isn't this step very costly? Yes, it is. It will cost you your favorite sins, the dirt on the carpet of your living room. Jesus is the man with the vacuum cleaner. It is His part to clean up the mess, yours to allow Him to do so. It is called "repentance" in the trade! To follow Jesus will cost you your sins, yes, and your self-centeredness too. Gradually you will be taken down several pegs and will acknowledge Jesus as boss in different areas of your life. It does not come overnight, this surrender and discipleship, but it is essential for Christian living. It will also cost you your secrecy. You see, it will not do to make a little private transaction with Jesus and hope nobody will notice. They will be bound to find out, if you are faithful to Him. And Jesus made it plain that if we would not confess Him before our fellow human beings He would not confess us before His heavenly Father. Hear St. Paul again:

> *"If you confess with your lips that Jesus is Lord, and believe in your heart that God raised him from the dead, you will be saved."*   (Romans 10:9)

Private belief and public confession are the two sides of the same coin. Yes, it is costly to become a Christian. But it is much more costly not to become one. That would mean no forgiveness, no joy, no fellowship with Christ and His people on earth, and no heaven. Very costly. A bit like getting married. You say farewell to the old life as you take on the new commitment and go public on it with a wedding ceremony and a ring you wear, without caring who sees it. Moreover you try to please your partner not because you have to but because you want to. It is like that with Jesus. And nobody looks back at the end of their life and says, "It was too costly to follow you, Jesus. It simply wasn't worth it!"

"Would it last?" you wonder. Yes. Not because you suddenly turn into Superman or woman, but because Christ promises that He will never fail you nor forsake you (Hebrews 13:5). That means He will never let you down and never give you up.

Perhaps you are asking yourself: *"How exactly could I start this relationship with Jesus Christ? It seems too absurdly simple just to ask Him to come into my life and take control."* It is simple but not absurdly so. Often people miss it because they try to make it too complicated. Think of it. When someone is adopted into a family, they have to sign a document accepting the offer, yes? When someone joins the army, they have to sign on, do they not? I have, as an Army officer, administered the oath of allegiance to many soldiers. They sign on, and from that moment on they are regular soldiers and have all the benefits and face all the challenges of their position. And of course it is like that when we get married. The clergyman or registrar asks the man, "Will you take this woman to have and to hold, for better or worse, for richer or poorer, until death parts you?" and the man replies, "I will." The same question is put to the bride, and she too replies, "I will." Then and not until then can the minister symbolically join their hands and declare them man and wife. In the old Prayer Book service he goes on to say, "What God has joined together let no man put asunder." A totally new relationship has begun: it is scheduled to last. That is a very good analogy to beginning the relationship with Jesus. We look to Him and ask, "Will you both forgive me and accept me into an intimate fellowship with You?" and He replies, "I will." We then have to decide whether we will take Him "for better or worse, for richer or poorer, until not even death can part us"! And once we do, it is indeed like marriage. And Christian baptism is like the ring in marriage: it is the physical mark of the start of this new life, which goes on getting better over the years.

This is not the place to explain about going on in the Christian life. I have tried to do so in my book *New Life, New Lifestyle* (Hodder). But think of the new soldier: he is going to draw his pay, his rifle and uniform and other benefits – but he is also going to have to undergo basic training (mercifully, not on his own but with others in the squad). Think of the new wife: she finds her husband's finances are hers to share, but she has to take his name and accommodate herself to his ways.

Discipleship involves drawing on Christ's strength, by asking for it when we need it. It involves putting on the uniform and unashamedly standing out for Christ and His values at work and home. It means discovering a group of other Christians to help in the early days of Christian living: the Alpha Course* is currently the best known and

---

* Alpha International Office
  E-mail: info@alphacourse.org
  Website: www.alphacourse.org

most widely available. And it will involve keeping in touch with the Lover you cannot see. How? Just as you would with any friend who lives far away. By e-mail or letter he tells you about who he is, how he can help, what you can do for him, and how much he loves you. And with Christ you can respond by picking up the phone of prayer – talking to Him about your joys and sorrows, your problems and the friends you want to introduce to Him. Those are some of the ways to grow in that relationship with Jesus. But it can't grow until it begins. You can't share your experiences with someone until you are introduced. You cannot be a spouse to someone until you have said those little words "I will". So how about it? Take your time. Reflect on the fact that Jesus Christ brings God to you and longs to bring you personally to God. He died on the cross to clear the way. He is alive to welcome you and to put His unseen Spirit into your heart, if only you will ask Him.

> *"Here I am! I stand at the door and knock. If anyone hears my voice and opens the door, I will come in . . . "*

Ask Him. Say something like this, only in your own words:

> "Jesus, I have kept you out too long. Please come in and bring me that intimacy with God which I can find nowhere else. Come in today. Come in to stay."

And then thank Him for coming, for He keeps His promises and if He said He would come in He *has* come in, provided you have asked Him. You may feel very different all at once. You may not. The important thing is that the relationship has begun, and you have all the rest of your life and eternity to develop it.

Ch 4/Oll

87 " " re: the fall of the whole
58+ 7L Easter Evidence
In Islam Jesus did—
Judas did

18 " " guilt

88 Rev 3:10 Heart turn
Jesus at el door Lll

86 14 Rev 5 "
now our

7L Buddhist
16 Prod Son
4/13
31 (30) Lk 14:15-24 W

30+ Phil 2:1f X
59 Jn 19:34 X
9 Easter